D0893364

THE FOUR DILEMMAS
OF THE CEO

THE FOUR DILEMMAS
OF THE CEO

*Mastering the make-or-break
moments in every executive's career*

TOM BIESINGER
ROSS WALL
CLIFFORD HERBERTSON

Bloomsbury Business
An imprint of Bloomsbury Publishing Plc

B L O O M S B U R Y
LONDON · OXFORD · NEW YORK · NEW DELHI · SYDNEY

Bloomsbury Business

An imprint of Bloomsbury Publishing Plc

50 Bedford Square
London
WC1B 3DP
UK

1385 Broadway
New York
NY 10018
USA

www.bloomsbury.com

BLOOMSBURY and the Diana logo are trademarks of Bloomsbury Publishing Plc

First published 2017

British Library Cataloguing-in-Publication Data
A catalogue record for this book is available from the British Library.

ISBN: HB: 978-1-4729-4684-3
ePDF: 978-1-4729-4683-6
ePub: 978-1-4729-4686-7

Library of Congress Cataloging-in-Publication Data
Names: Biesinger, Tom, author. | Wall, Ross, author.
Title: The four dilemmas of the CEO : mastering the make-or-break moments in every
executive's career / by Tom Biesinger and Ross Wall.
Description: London ; New York, NY : Bloomsbury Business, 2017. |
Includes bibliographical references and index. Identifiers:
LCCN 2016057184 (print) | LCCN 2017014636 (ebook) | ISBN 9781472946836 (ePDF) |
ISBN 9781472946867 (ePub) | ISBN 9781472946843 (hardback)
Subjects: LCSH: Chief executive officers. | Executives. | Career development.
Classification: LCC HD38.2 (ebook) | LCC HD38.2 .B53 2017 (print) |
DDC658.4/2–dc23
LC record available at https://lccn.loc.gov/2016057184

Cover design by Eleanor Rose
Cover image © Getty Images

Typeset by Integra Software Services Pvt. Ltd.
Printed and bound in Great Britain

CONTENTS

FOREWORD

Historically, there have been two fundamentally different views of God: one view is that God exists *above* the universe and, like Zeus, is able to cause anything to happen by simply pointing His finger. The second view is that God exists *within* the universe, and that His omnipotence comes from His omniscience. In other words, His power comes from His perfect understanding of the laws of the universe and His ability to harness those laws.

These two fundamentally different views exist for CEOs too. One view of the CEO is that she, like Zeus, causes things to happen with a simple snap of her fingers. Give the order, and it's done. The other view of the CEO is that she is powerful because she understands and can harness the forces, constraints, vectors, and processes inside and outside her company.

I subscribe to this second view of the CEO. As a result, in my own research I have sought to develop theories of management—statements of what causes what and why—to try to help executives understand the causal mechanisms working in their 'universe' that they must harness to succeed.

Not all theories are created alike. Good theory must be circumstance-contingent, meaning it must show what circumstances and conditions need to be present for its statement of cause and effect to still hold (and, conversely, the conditions under which the outcome will be different). Having a circumstance-contingent theory enables leaders to understand what it is about their present situation that enabled their strategies and tactics to succeed in the past. And it also enables leaders to recognize when important circumstances in their environment are shifting, so they can change course and sustain their success in the future.

This is especially crucial for CEOs, who face dramatically different circumstances throughout their tenures. Being able to identify and respond to these changing circumstances is no easy task; but it is this ability that separates the great CEOs from the mediocre.

I often say in jest to executives that if they are overwhelmed with the demands of their job, they can always just become an academic like me—because academics merely have to *talk* about things; CEOs have to actually *do* them. However, if like many of them you insist on remaining a CEO, then do yourself a favor and read this book. It will reveal the dilemmas you will face during your tenure, provide you sage advice on how to overcome them, and help you achieve sustainable success.

Professor Clayton M. Christensen
Harvard Business School, 2017

An invitation

CEOs hate surprises!

And yet many CEOs (in fact, most of them in our experience) have at some point in their careers found themselves surprised by make-or-break moments they should have seen coming.

There are four such moments, which we call *The Four Dilemmas of the CEO*. These are consistent across all industries and across all enterprises of notable size, regardless of geography. They follow a very reliable pattern over a CEO's life cycle, a pattern that has never before been captured in print.

Here in this book we outline for you these most predictable inflection points in the life of a CEO. While the specifics differ, we will show you the common challenges every CEO faces during their tenure and when to expect them. Once you understand these dilemmas and what causes them, you can take action to overcome them.

The purpose of this book is to help you navigate these inevitable challenges that can cause paralysis and stall critical momentum. Once you've digested what we offer here, these career-limiting dilemmas won't come as a surprise, and you will be able to break through the self-imposed glass ceilings that cause CEOs to lose momentum and get stuck *in* their business rather than working *on* it.

The biggest danger of all to any top executive is irrelevancy. As a CEO, momentum is your most precious possession. With it you can accomplish anything. Without it, it's game over. Your tenure will be cut short, and your reputation will be tainted.

Jim Fallon is a former Scottish footballer who went on to manage Dumbarton F.C., Scotland's fourth oldest football club. Although he was a capable player during his years on the field, Fallon's stint as Dumbarton's manager secured his place in history as one of the worst managers in the history of the game.

At the start of the 1995 season, Dumbarton was on a roll, having won its first two matches. That momentum abruptly stalled, however, when Jim Fallon was brought in to replace departing manager Murdo MacLeod an hour before their third match.

Upon appointing Fallon manager, Dumbarton promptly lost the match 0–4. This humiliating loss marked the start of a trend: of the thirty-four matches remaining that season, Dumbarton would win only one, scoring fewer goals in all thirty-four matches than they had in their first two without Fallon.

Displaying a faith in him that bordered on the religious and with the sting of relegation still freshly lingering in the air, the club inexplicably offered Fallon a new contract for the following season.

Determination notwithstanding, the following season was no better: Dumbarton played twelve more matches with Fallon in charge, losing eight of them and winning only one. By the time he departed in November of 1996, Fallon's record for the forty-six matches Dumbarton played under his fourteen-month reign would have shamed a youth league team at the World Cup: two wins, five draws, and thirty-nine losses. The result of this dismal performance? The team suffered two straight seasons of relegation to a lower division due to its bottom-ranked season finishes, going from Scotland's First Division to its Third Division in merely one year and two months. Dumbarton's selection of an inexperienced manager and Fallon's acceptance of a job for which he was unqualified destroyed the team's momentum and permanently damaged his professional reputation, relegating the club to Division Three and Fallon to irrelevance.

Momentum is your most prized possession. Your legacy will be forged through the building and sustaining of momentum, ensuring that the bulk of your tenure is spent working *on* the business instead of getting stuck *in* it. So what creates momentum in the first place? Momentum arises from the proper balance of *relevance* and *conviction*. Simply put, *relevance* is how badly the business needs you, and *conviction* is how badly you need the business.

Today's CEOs[1] are under immense pressure. It has never been tougher for them—they face intense board engagement, activist investors, a war raging for their talent, dynamic and unpredictable markets, unseen and unknown competition, blurred value chains, unprecedented public scrutiny, and regulatory transparency.

It is not going to get any easier.

CEOs no longer enjoy the luxury of maintaining the status quo, providing incremental returns, or simply defending market share. They must create massive momentum by focusing *on* their businesses with a loyal and competent team that can continually innovate, create sustainable breakthrough results, and shape future markets.

We understand from first-hand experience that being a CEO is a tough, lonely, stressful job that most people can't even imagine. Despite having earned their status by obtaining unquestionable results with relentless dedication, and despite having thrived in Darwinian environments, it still is a constant battle to remain relevant. The effort to maintain the conviction necessary to stay at the top comes at a huge price for the enterprises, and for the CEOs themselves.

One of the great ironies CEOs face is that, although they interact with people constantly, they are also entirely alone, with few peers and fewer confidants. Spouses and friends offer empathy but are rarely in a position to provide true guidance. There are too few places for a CEO to turn for real help or insight.

It has been our privilege to guide hundreds of CEOs and their executive committees. We have worked in a variety of sectors across the globe, in businesses that are larger than some nations. We have worked beside these people as their trusted advisors and assisted them throughout their entire life cycles, from new appointees to seasoned veterans building lasting legacies. We have helped shape individuals, and we have aided in the delivery of destinies.

We have never marketed our services nor revealed our roles. Instead, we have perfected our craft in anonymity, content knowing that our role is not to be kings. Our role is to be the people behind the throne who make sure that the king's reign is successful from start to finish.

Our own dilemma in writing this book has been how to share the wisdom we have gained while protecting the privacy of the people we have served. We are not researchers, professors, or—until now—authors, just seasoned professionals whose knowledge was forged in the crucible of experience.

We have learned by doing, by honing our craft with titans of industry, and we must honor their trust. We fully understand the potential consequences of "stepping out from behind the pillars of power" into full view, and we have deliberately chosen not to use "name and shame" examples that would violate the trust we are proud to have earned.

In these pages, we will offer you insights that will benefit you wherever you are on your path—a new CEO at the beginning of an ambitious tenure, an established CEO unsure how to grow the company to a breakthrough level, or a veteran CEO determining what to do next after an incredibly successful career.

Most CEOs we know have stopped reading books, especially of this nature, relying instead on short articles about relevant current events. We get it. It's not the time invested but the lack of value derived! We have not watered down our core message to the lowest common denominator; we describe and discuss exactly what we know. We have distilled as much value as we know how into these pages. We have scrutinized every word and pored over every sentence to ensure that each page generates insight and sharpens your intuition.

Our promise to you is that we have given the writing of this book our best effort and fully expect you to find massive value within its pages. Please consider the contents of this book as a gift from us to you.

We invite you to thoughtfully consider our framework, perhaps recognize one or more of these dilemmas in your own professional life, and allow us to show you how to navigate them successfully.

The easiest way to survive a disaster is to avert it entirely, knowing that it was coming, instead of allowing it to arrive as an unwelcome surprise.

Until now we've never publicly shared our wisdom. But we believe the time is right for us to pass along some of our insights. In doing so, it is our sincere hope that these pages will enable CEOs everywhere to create the momentum necessary to build businesses that are Market Shapers and Talent Makers.

We trust that these pages will assist you not only in building momentum, but also in showing you how to accomplish more than you ever thought possible.

−Tom, Ross, and Clifford

1

Introducing the CEO life cycle

The most common complaint we hear from CEOs when we first start working with them is "I don't even have time to think."

How much time do you spend working *in* the business versus working *on* the business?

If you are like many CEOs, your answer is that you spend the majority of your time working *in* the business: making decisions for others, weighing options, pointing out pitfalls, sorting out political catfights, arbitrating territorial disputes, securing next quarter's numbers, reporting results, and managing shareholder challenges. In short, you are spending far too much valuable time managing noise and doing your direct reports' and board's jobs for them!

Is working *in* the business really what the board hired you to do? You've got (or had) a small amount of grace while you "settle in," but you know the honeymoon will soon be over. In our experience, every hour you spend working *in* the business on the front end, during your initial grace period, will cost you three hours of working *on* the business on the back end. That's because results take time and have a tail before you can bank them. Let's be very clear: You were hired to work *on* the business. That is the CEO's job. If you are spending less than 75 percent of your time working *on* the business, your relevance and conviction will be at serious risk and you will be putting your future and the organization's future in jeopardy.

The CEOs we work with often find this problem deeply frustrating. They've finally made it to the top, but they are handling trivialities instead of moving an enterprise forward. How do you move past the babysitting function and do what you were hired to do?

The purpose of mapping out the CEO life cycle is to help you recognize when you are stuck or are about to get stuck, guide you to predict what is coming next, and accelerate you through to your next likely challenge. In our experience, there is a direct cause-and-effect relationship between the four dilemmas and your life cycle as a CEO. Highly successful CEOs move swiftly and adeptly through the life cycle and the related dilemmas. Less successful CEOs get stuck and hit self-made ceilings at each dilemma.

The following illustration represents the four life-cycle phases of a CEO; this model will be referred to often throughout the book as we offer the keys to moving through the CEO dilemmas—so a brief explanation at this juncture should prove helpful.[1]

The model represents the life cycle of a CEO within the context of his current role. When a CEO moves to another organization, he starts over at the beginning of the life cycle.[2] We know that our readers are at various phases in the life cycle and that certain phases we describe will resonate with their current circumstances more than others. That's intentional—there's something here for everyone and we're sure you'll recognize it.

The Y-axis of the model measures a CEO's relevance to the organization and its main stakeholders. When CEOs first take up their roles, they must prove themselves; as they continue to do so, their relevance increases.

The X-axis of the model measures conviction. As CEOs navigate successfully through the life cycle phases, their conviction grows. If they are unsuccessful they stall, and their tenure is cut short.

The four phases of the life cycle are hierarchical in nature, although a CEO initially faces the combined noise of all the dilemmas. Successful CEOs navigate their life cycles through focused discipline: addressing Dilemma One without getting caught up in the commotion of Dilemmas Two through Four; knowing that by successfully addressing Dilemma One, they will earn the time and space to focus on the next phase and *its* associated dilemma.

The model builds from bottom left to right, starting with minimal relevance and heightening conviction.

In Phase One of the model, you are faced with Dilemma One, during which time your emphasis is mainly on determining *what* your real focus should be.

During Phase Two of the model, as relevance and conviction grow, you are faced with navigating Dilemma Two: determining *who* your team will be.

Next comes Dilemma Three: *how* to create sustainable breakthrough.

The fourth and final phase of the life cycle brings with it Dilemma Four: constant realignment to your own very personal *why*.

The shaded sections are an indication of the recommended balance of time you and your Executive Committee (ExCo) must maintain between working *in* the business and working *on* the business.

The white line represents the trajectory of your momentum. As relevance and conviction (the business's need for you and your need for the business) increase, your momentum will trend upward. A dip in either axis can lead to stalling or getting stuck, and if not addressed will lead to your decline and departure.

If you fail to have adequate personal renewal and miss the opportunity to reinvent yourself prior to the next dilemma challenge, you will experience a trough after each dilemma peak. Continual personal renewal and timely reinvention is required of all CEOs, in order to counter burnout and restore the energy required to tackle each of the four dilemmas.

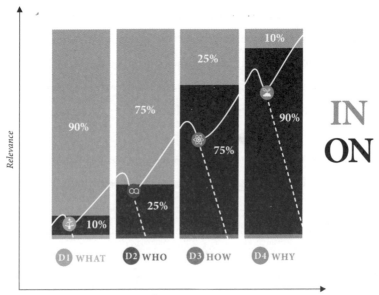

The moment you take office, the hourglass is overturned and the intense, unforgiving scrutiny begins. Should your performance dip below the expectations of your paymasters, a ready supply of ambitious competitors (some perhaps less qualified than you) waits to replace you or even engineer your demise. You can't afford a misstep. You can't even afford a learning curve. Every delay, every impediment will bring you one step closer to the end of your tenure.

The World Series is on the line, Boston against New York. An easy out means victory and a costly error upends the results.

Thinking Bill Buckner and the 1986 Fall Classic?

Think again.

Thirty-seven years before Bill Buckner was born, an eerily similar situation took place in the World Series of 1912.

The combatants were the Red Sox (appropriately enough) and the New York Giants.

The seventh game of the Series ended in a tie, called because of darkness.

So the Series, tied at three games apiece, went to a conclusive eighth game.

The Giants were up by a run in the ninth inning when Fred Snodgrass, a catcher-turned-outfielder, camped out under a routine fly ball that would have been an easy second out. He had made the play a thousand times, and felt confident that he could pull it off with ease as he reached skyward nonchalantly with one hand, and dropped it.

The Red Sox suddenly had a second life, which they capitalized on by plating two runners, taking the lead, and ultimately winning the game and the crown.

Fred Snodgrass had committed the sin of overconfidence—of not giving 100 percent of his effort to the play because he didn't think he needed to. The result affected his entire legacy. Instead of being remembered for his many accomplishments, Fred never escaped the infamy of that one lapse in judgment. When he passed away in 1974, more than sixty years after the mistake, his *New York Times* obituary bore the headline, "Fred Snodgrass, 86, Dead; Ball Player Muffed 1912 Fly."

Similarly, Mickey Owen, a respected Brooklyn Dodgers catcher, is remembered for allowing what would have been the last pitch of the 1941 World Series to scoot underneath him. He is remembered for single-handedly giving the Yankees an unexpected Series win.

And the aforementioned Bill Buckner enjoyed a great baseball career prior to his own moment of infamy, when he missed a routine ground ball that shot between his legs and into right field, allowing the second-base runner to score the winning run. (Ironically, his manager had made a fatal mistake of his own: leaving Bill on the field so that he could experience first-hand the last pitch of a World Series victory.)

We think you understand our point. Whether it's fair or not, a few big mistakes can overshadow all our right choices and definitive successes. This is as true in business as it is in sports. But understanding the four dilemmas and reacting to them effectively can keep you from committing unnecessary errors and falling foul. This understanding will ensure your success as a CEO and safeguard your hard-won legacy.

***

Before we go into each dilemma in greater depth, we want to offer an overview of the CEO life cycle and the attendant challenges that arise along the way. Our overarching belief is that the crisis points CEOs face are entirely predictable. They are not industry-specific or a function of economic conditions. Rather, they are inevitable—and forewarned, of course, is forearmed.

So we begin with the first dilemma.

You're ready to get started. You've been hired for a reason. You walk in the door on your first day with exactly what the company needs: conviction. You have done your due diligence. You have clear ideas about what you need to accomplish, and you're eager to prove to the board that they've made the right choice.

Now you need to make things happen.

What if things don't happen as quickly as they should? You have meetings, you make speeches, you share your vision, and you map out strategic plans. You review metrics with different members of your executive committee and everyone seems to agree with your ideas (or they say they do), but you aren't seeing the pace you need. Worse, you keep getting different information from different people—sometimes conflicting information—and you don't have a good way to know which data to believe. Your ambitious goals are getting trampled under the he-said/she-saids, and you find yourself spending too much time trying to triangulate contradictory information just to get a basic understanding of what's going on in your own company. You don't know what or whom to trust, and you aren't clear how best to move forward.

Does this sound familiar? We hear this from our new clients every day.

You may have great conviction, but at this early phase in your tenure, you do not yet have great relevance within the company. You are still learning how things work around the place; you're still learning where the bodies are buried; and in practice, it's your executive committee that is in control, not you.

This is the first dilemma of the CEO: *You are in charge of everything, but cannot completely trust anything*.

It's not just a problem that affects new CEOs, though every new CEO faces it. It is an issue faced by every CEO struggling for traction at any stage in his or her career. If you can't overcome this dilemma, you will suffer the pains of irrelevancy.

The good news is that once you understand the problem and what's causing it, the solution is within your grasp—and here it is: *You must set a single agenda, your own agenda. The Agenda.* This means crushing all competing agendas that distract the organization, create noise, or obscure the clarity of your direction and message.

You must align your organization with your goals from the top down. You must define in clear, unambiguous, and measurable terms what you want, what you expect, and what is unacceptable—and then hold your executive committee accountable for delivery. They, in turn, need to understand that each of them, top to bottom, will be evaluated and judged based on how they progress, measurably, within The Agenda. Those who align themselves with it will be rewarded, and those who don't will face the consequences.

When you set The Agenda clearly, you are giving every member of your executive team an opportunity to demonstrate whether he or she is falling in line or falling on one side of it or the other: in or out.

This will give you a clear picture of who is potentially on your team and who definitely isn't; whom you can pull closer and whom you need to distance yourself from; and finally, who will help you get things done and who will get in the way.

Let's define some terms. A *formal agenda* is what you are happy to publish for public consumption. It focuses on what you actually intend to do during your tenure as CEO. The formal agenda, however, is very seldom the actual agenda. The *informal agenda* is how you choose to allocate your scarce resources and talent to actively achieve your agreed-upon mandate. The informal agenda can create a strong emotional response in executives, so it is often not widely shared. The informal agenda includes details about whom you intend to use and in what capacity. These decisions are initially based on alignment and loyalty, with the most significant roles going to those who are the most widely trusted.

Setting The Agenda is the first step in increasing your relevance within the organization, and doing it resolves the CEO's dilemma of being unable to get reliable information or make good progress toward goals.

But this soon leads to another problem.

For better or worse, the most loyal members of your executive committee—the ones who have proved that they will get behind The Agenda in tangible, measurable ways—aren't always the most competent people in the organization. This is natural. The executives who are best at what they do may also be the most resistant to change. They've figured out how to be successful at their own jobs without you, and they know as well as you do that CEOs generally don't last more than a handful of years. Maybe they wanted your job but didn't get it, or were loyal to your predecessor and see your potential failure as their opportunity. Why should they risk their own careers when the easier alternative might be to wait out your tenure instead?

So the people who drive the most revenue, the people with the most valuable knowledge or contacts, may also be the ones who are least eager to get on board with you.

This creates the CEO's second dilemma: *You know today's executive cannot deliver tomorrow's results.*

Which is most important: loyalty or competence? Ultimately, you want—and will demand—both. But most CEOs make the mistake of believing that they can have both right from the start. Not so. You must choose one, and the wrong choice could prove fatal.

If you can figure out how to balance loyalty and competence, you will create massive momentum within your business. You will achieve more than just your mandate. You will broaden your reach within the organization, strengthen your reputation with the board, and you will be given greater freedom to achieve even better results.

But if you can't get the balance right, you will wind up either yoked to loyal people who may not be capable of meeting the challenges ahead or competing with extraordinarily able people who may not be willing to work toward The Agenda. Ideally, of course, you want both loyalty and competence—but you want them *in that order*, because with resistant people, it is impossible to create the momentum you need.

To help CEOs navigate this dilemma, we have created a rubric that has proved invaluable in decision-making. We call it *Organizational Quotient*, or *OQ*. Simply put, OQ helps you identify and select your executive committee and key executive talent across the business and then rely on those people to align and mobilize a motivated workforce. OQ will help you determine how to accelerate organizational alignment and where and when to delegate your power, and ensure that each member of your team is contributing to The Agenda. One of the main benefits of OQ is capacity generation; for you, for your executive, and for the organization.

Once the framework of OQ is clear to the executive committee, each of them is empowered to become a higher-functioning member of the enterprise, working at full capacity to achieve The Agenda. A CEO who understands OQ and has embedded it in the organization has fully capitalized on his or her conviction in order to maximize relevance within the organization. Surrounded by a team of highly competent people working loyally towards The Agenda, this CEO is powerful indeed.

Once you've settled in, surrounded yourself with a great team, and aligned everyone with The Agenda, you are at the peak of your relevance as a CEO. This is when you are best able to deliver on the promises you made to the board and even exceed them. Problems come up now and then—internal disputes, threats from competitors, acts of God—but your team is capable and prepared, and you all react in step to quash any setback. Things are running smoothly.

Perhaps ... too smoothly.

At this point in your career, the temptation can be strong to settle in, stick with the routines that work, and not upset the apple cart. After all, you've worked hard every minute of every day for decades to get where you are. You've hit your stride. The job actually seems easy now, and you just want to rest for bit and enjoy the fact that your business works as well as it does. You want to take a little victory lap. Why not? After all, you've earned it.

This is the point in your life cycle when your conviction may begin to wane.

The drive that got you to where you are may be weakening. You may find that your inclination, and that of everyone around you, is to limit your risk by shifting from offense to defense, gathering your returns, and continuing to do exactly what you've been doing. At best, you might pursue small, incremental, low-risk improvements.

This brings about the third dilemma of the CEO: *How do you engage the full capability of your executive on the business when their reputations were earned working in the business?*

The status quo of incremental performance is an illusion. The market is going to change and it's going to change rapidly, so you can never let up. If you stop in an attempt to entrench, fortify, and protect the gains you've made, your competitors will invariably continue to innovate—fiercely—and you will lose what you have built. You must innovate fiercely, too, or you will be left behind.

So you have built a company and aligned it according to The Agenda, and you've assembled and encouraged a team of people you trust to work with you to achieve The Agenda—and they've done it. They've achieved everything that you've asked of them.

But intuitively you know there's more.

What do you do?

To remain relevant and neutralize global challenges, you must continue to innovate. There is no time for a victory lap. This is not the time for risk aversion, and there are no laurels upon which to rest. You can't create breakthroughs without taking risk. You can't be afraid to do something that has never been done before—because if you do nothing, you'll be displaced or replaced for sure.

All your prior successes were based on offense, on innovation, on pushing forward boldly—and this time is no different. But it's also *entirely* different, because innovation, by definition, requires you to be different each and every time.

It is time to create a *sustainable breakthrough*—but what is it? Where do breakthrough ideas come from? Can breakthrough become a discipline? Is management the enemy of creativity? Is expertise becoming a commodity? How do enterprises stay competitive in the global marketplace amid ruthless competition? Is breakthrough the sole responsibility of the CEO, a lone genius?

To create a sustainable breakthrough, you have to change everything. You have to change the way you think, what you measure, and even the way you innovate. You can't do it by yourself; if you want to reconceive your company, you have to get your executive committee on board. It must be a collaborative effort. You need to leverage their collective capability.

Sustainable breakthrough is more than just astounding results. It is the right combination of breakthrough results, breakthrough leadership, and a healthy breakthrough environment. Achieving this kind of breakthrough is how a CEO passes through this third dilemma. It requires activating the executive committee, transforming them from experts who are highly functional only in their particular verticals into well-rounded, commercially astute leaders who work *on* the business. Contribution is no longer individual; it's collective. The CEO empowers the executive committee to create and drive sustainable breakthrough.

Most CEOs never get past Dilemma Three because the CEO and ExCo themselves don't fully comprehend their own potential; they believe they were hired as functional experts only, and nothing more. This belief all but guarantees that the CEO and the ExCo can add only incremental value to the enterprise and must settle for marginal gains and an occasional success story that will become urban legend.

For the limited number of CEOs who choose to tackle this dilemma, the benefits of capability engagement really begin to kick in—especially since they will have top-graded their executive with the best talent they can find: the *A players*. Only with this abundance of aligned talent will the CEO have the ability to generate breakthrough outcomes year after year. Without an ExCo filled with A players, the CEO and the organization will continue to be limited by the CEO's own creativity and longevity.

An A player is loyal and competent at his role, adds enterprise-wide value, and has the potential to do your job in the immediate term. An A player has a high-level OQ, doesn't require air cover or cleanup, and actively manages results by constantly looking up for alignment. In contrast, a *B player* is a loyal specialist or functional expert capable of doing his job, but he struggles to add value enterprise-wide. B players are more concerned with managing perceptions of their individual brands; they lack the discipline to constantly look up for alignment and adjust to achieve the needed results.

BALTIMORE COUNTY PUBLIC LIBRARY

WhiteMarsh Branch
410-887-5097
www.bcpl.info

Customer ID: **********0372

Items that you checked out

Title: For the love of money : a memoir
ID: 31183181931913
Due: Thursday, October 04, 2018
Messages:
Item checkout ok. You just saved $25.00 by
using your library today.

Title:
 The four dilemmas of the CEO : mastering
 the make-or-break moments in every
 executive's career
ID: 31183188013848
Due: Thursday, October 04, 2018
Messages:
Item checkout ok. You just saved $30.00 by
using your library today.

Total items: 2
Account balance: $0.00
9/13/2018 8:58 AM
Checked out: 2
Overdue: 0
Hold requests: 0
Ready for pickup: 0
Messages:
Patron status is ok.

HOMEWORK HELP

Brainfuse tutoring, Rosetta Stone,

research databases and more

Available at bcpl.info

The CEO who has identified this dilemma now knows his former playbook won't bring him the breakthrough results he desires. The CEO who believes he is capable of breakthrough innovation surrounds himself with A players. All players must be A players or well on their way to that status. The CEO cannot allow his most valuable fields to lie fallow because of an investment he failed to make. Investing in the future by hiring A players and pointing their collective attitudes toward sustainable breakthrough takes time and consideration to yield results; the full force and focus of the ExCo must be *on* the business.

Breakthrough collaboration is one of the most difficult leadership traits to master, and when it comes to fruition—when the CEO is able to mobilize a high-performance workforce and harness their collective efforts—the results are extremely powerful.

When faced with the opportunity to enjoy the status quo, the best CEOs do exactly the opposite: They innovate more deeply and intensely than ever. They embrace the unknown with dogged persistence. And they require the same commitment to innovation from their executive committee, preparing each member to make the transition from functional expert to commercially astute leader, so that they may someday make their own transition into the CEO role. They break the marketplace and take it somewhere it's never been—and they do it over and over, time and again, shaping their marketplace and the world.

This leads straight to the fourth dilemma: ***At what point does the price of remaining personally relevant outweigh your other options?***

Being a CEO is demanding. The job occupies nearly all of your waking hours, and these aren't easy hours. Your every decision is scrutinized. Every sentence you utter, even off-handedly, can send your stock price tumbling. Your competitors want to crush you and your "colleagues" want your job. Disaster can come at any moment, from any direction, and it often does, threatening to knock your plans off the rails. You miss your child's dance recitals, if not her entire childhood. You have to cancel the reservations for your anniversary dinner—that is, if you are fortunate enough that your spouse hasn't divorced you over all the dinners you missed in the past.

But when your conviction is waning, you ask yourself, what now? What next? Are you really willing to go through all of this over and over again? And, more important, how? How are you going to find it in yourself to start over and innovate again? How do you reinvent yourself in order to remain relevant?

When you can no longer innovate, you begin to adopt defensive strategies instead. You push others away. You eliminate any challengers who might threaten your position—perhaps even trusted lieutenants with whom you have gone into battle for years. Mismatched momentum always ends poorly.

When CEOs fail to reinvent but continue to hold on, the enterprise suffers. But less obviously, so does the CEO, because his personal and professional needs are no longer being met. What is the personal and organizational cost of a CEO hanging on? If the company spends too much time in this state, decline sets in and everyone suffers.

There is only one way to pass through this fourth dilemma, and that is the intersection of your ongoing *renewal* process and consistent *reinvention*. You must rediscover your passion and follow it wherever it takes you.

Powerful people find reinvention challenging because there are so many incentives to cling to the old ways. The quest starts with a seemingly simple question: Should you stay or should you go? Whatever your choice, it requires alignment between what is important to you—your internal *why*—and what is exciting to you, which needs continual recalibration. If you stay, you must find a way to reinvent yourself, to create conviction and relevance again—because once the conviction is gone, the game is over. You must ask of yourself the same thing you have asked of your company all these years: innovation. You must identify your real priorities and values in order to define your new set of options and then map out your next steps. That is the only way to stay relevant.

Sooner or later, you will reach the end, the point at which you don't have the conviction to innovate again. You know you're capable, but it will simply cost you too much. You will decide to go. This road isn't easy either, because it also requires reinvention. Transitioning from life as a CEO—one of the most powerful humans on the planet— to something else can be an enormous shock, but it can also be enormously rewarding. There is life after the pressure-filled days, but only if you prepare properly for it.

But before you can even think that far down the road, you must establish your agenda, "The Agenda" for your organization, lest others set their own agendas and distract you from fulfilling your mandate. What your tenure will be known for is the subject of our next chapter.

2

The first dilemma

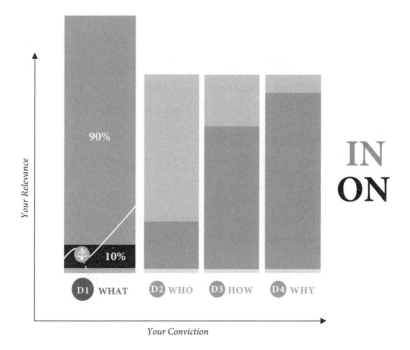

As we all know, most CEOs do not initially choose their executive teams; they inherit them.

The first few weeks of a CEO's tenure usually serve as an exploratory phase for the CEO and executive alike. Prior to the initial meeting, all will have done their due diligence on one another, but no amount of information about past performance can be a reliable predictor of future benefit for either party. This grace period is the time for the CEO to take inventory of the size and scope of the task at hand. This unique window also provides a clear view of who *not* to take on the journey; individuals move from being question marks in the CEO's mind to exclamation points in his heart.

As a CEO, you need to understand right off the bat that organizations are not necessarily as they appear. If you hope to accomplish anything, you must quickly and accurately diagnose and fix the issues influencing personalities, attitudes, and strategic business needs. With insight comes understanding of what needs to be done, and the ability to see through the games of corporate hide-and-seek so you can set things right. If you are a new CEO or just experiencing a lack of traction, you are encountering the first dilemma of the CEO life cycle:

You are in charge of everything, but cannot completely trust anything.

Every CEO has what we jokingly call a "fowl problem": the feathers vs. the chicken. The whole bird is yours to grab, and it seems plump—but how do you know how much bird you really have and how much of it is just feathers? A CEO's day is filled with decisions, most of which are monumental—and they all depend on access to timely, reliable advice and information. But when you grab for the information, you need to be able to tell the bird from the feathers.

A CEO's information generally comes from the executive committee and their direct reports, and it's important to remember that this information is rarely unbiased. Each member of the executive team is responsible for a particular vertical, and he is evaluated (and compensated) based on the performance of that vertical. These are smart, ambitious people—so why would you expect them to present information that might make them look bad? Why wouldn't they spin the information in their favor? In fact, you probably have done so a time or two yourself.

As a result, the information a CEO receives can be unreliable at worst or hard to decipher at best. It may even be contradictory. Members of the team may be rewriting history to take advantage of your ignorance (this all happened before your time) and further their own agendas. Those who attempt to provide you with unsolicited advice early in the game are probably attempting to draw you near. These team members may be trying to demonstrate alignment, but they are not necessarily competent.

The real threats are still sizing you up. In most instances, they would be quite happy for you to fall on your own sword, so not much comes from their lips; they have no loyalty to you at this juncture. If they do speak, it is generally to answer a direct question or to pose one that might reveal your lack of knowledge.

It may seem that the best way to get reliable information would be to ask three different people the same question, cross-reference the answers, and triangulate a path to the truth. We encourage the discipline of corroborating data; the problem arises when you must burn precious time because you don't trust those providing the data. As you know the shortest path between two points is never a triangle.

As a CEO who is trying to do what's best for the company, you don't want to spend a lot of time and energy triangulating, trying to figure out what's going on and how to proceed.

That's no way to run a business.

When we ask CEOs in this phase of the life cycle to describe their goals for their organizations, they speak passionately and energetically about big ideas, long-term strategies, upcoming innovations, and market disruptions.

Then we ask them to describe their tasks during a typical workweek and their tenor changes. Most of their days, it turns out, aren't spent working toward these lofty goals at all. Most days are spent managing people—wrangling the wills of various members of the executive committee, who are in a constant state of bickering and infighting. The CEO sits at the center of this ego-maelstrom, settling turf wars, placating, brokering side-deals, trading off encouragement with corrective action—also known as babysitting—all just to get everyone to play nice and get to work on the real business at hand: the business.

In an effort to ascertain key data points, a newly appointed CEO begins to interrogate systems and executives to understand the breadth and depth of the challenge. Unfortunately, many new CEOs quickly focus on resolving key issues in the business—putting out fires. Every time you put on your firefighter's uniform and deal with operational issues, you get dragged further and further from the real task of taking the company in a bold new direction. Let others put out the fires. Your real task is to further The Agenda. Let others play defense; you must lead the offense. Once your team is in place, you can comfortably and safely move from the role of firefighter to that of chief executive. But how do you get to that point?

Winning Olympic Gold—Finally

Nine years of rowing with no Olympic medals to show for it and a horrifying eighth-place finish in Atlanta in 1996 sent the British men eights' rowing team into a tailspin. Great Britain had not won the event since 1912, and they knew they had to do something radical if they wanted to start winning.

How'd they pull it off?

The top rowers recognized that they had to focus on *one single goal* that would govern all of their behavior: *making the boat go faster.* Nothing else mattered.

The team was made up of a variety of personality types, each with his own habits and routines, but they all wanted to win. It was clear that wasting time on their differences, chiding and goading one another, was not going to make the boat go faster. Accordingly, the key change they made was to learn to trust and respect one another. They learned to give and receive feedback honestly and respect one another's differences. The task of transforming a group of individuals into a highly functional team is not an easy one. Here are some of the things the Olympic rowers did to make that happen:

1   They asked hard questions, because the nature of the task was exceedingly hard: Win Olympic Gold.

2   They continually varied their warm-up routines to expose preferences, weaknesses, and strengths.

3   Feedback was shared openly with the single goal: Win Olympic Gold.

4   The best idea always won.

5   They understood that daily hard work slowly shaped them into a more efficient machine that wasted no energy, and that would ultimately set them apart as winners.

6   They were resolute, vowing never to make the same mistake twice.

7   Their prevailing strategy never changed: Go really fast for the first 1,000 m ... and *even faster* for the second.

8   They understood that they didn't have to think alike or even like one another; their strength as a team could come from their differences, as long as they maintained mutual respect and a belief that each one was a key part of the best eights crew in the world.

9   They had absolute knowledge of the task at hand and what needed to be done. They could visualize the result; all they needed to do was make it happen, one stroke at a time.

10   They learned to trust implicitly and totally that each team member would do his individual part for the collective result: winning Olympic Gold.

So here's our question for you: is everyone on *your* team pulling in the same direction?

The opposite situation is misalignment, by which we mean an executive team with various competing agendas. Sadly, misalignment is business-as-usual at most companies. C-level executives are encouraged to be willful and authoritative about their turf, leaving the CEO to arbitrate, and most CEOs accept this as an essential part of the job.

But it's not essential. It's not even a part of the job at all. The CEO is hired by the board to deliver a mandate with specific results, not to spend his tenure mediating internal turf wars. Wasting a CEO's time and energy this way is truly a case of the tail wagging the dog. A CEO focused on internal politics and personalities is unable to focus on the real task at hand: renovating the enterprise and moving it forward.

Imagine how much more effective a CEO can be when his or her executive committee is uniformly aligned around a shared set of goals. This is not a pipe dream; it is entirely possible. In fact, we believe it's the only condition under which a CEO can be effective. In our experience, most CEOs spend upward of 80 percent of their time working *in* the business instead of being free to focus *on* the business, as they have been mandated to do. This is a poor use of expensive resources. Once a CEO has worked through Dilemmas One and Two, he is spending minimal time and effort managing misalignment and execution. This is essential, because the rest of the time needs to be devoted to winning.

To understand how to get to this point, let's first talk about misalignment itself.

What causes misalignment?

Misalignment happens when the members of an executive committee are pursuing different agendas instead of collaborating on a single one, The Agenda. Too many companies fracture because of misalignment. Tiny tiffs and disagreements among members of the executive committee eventually work their way down the entire organizational chart, growing into massive chasms that divide talent, burn resources, stifle communication, and confuse priorities. Whole divisions of the enterprise wind up pointed in different and even opposing directions, confusing colleagues for foes, and taking the fight internal instead of winning in the marketplace.

For you, this is a time to take note, to learn about your executive under pressure, without their masks on. Mostly they will be fighting one another. Observe their behavior and attitude; who smells blood and goes for more, who gangs up on whom, who rewrites history in his favor, who acts first and gets permission later, who waits to pounce, and so on. Take inventory of these incidents so you can utilize them at the right time, when you need to shape the behavior and attitudes of *your* team with your observations.

Misalignment has two main causes: *distraction* and *ambition*. They are equally destructive, and either or both can ruin a CEO's momentum.

Distraction generally stems from a lack of clarity. If the executive committee is unclear on the CEO's agenda, how to pursue it, and why it is better for them, they are likely to fall back on what is known and safe instead. Faced with uncertainty and change, most dig in their heels in a shortsighted attempt to generate stability. They leverage knowledge or key relationships to swim upstream against the agreed-upon agenda, defaulting to what they believe is best for the organization (which, in reality, is usually best for their personal agenda).

A member of the executive committee may want to demonstrate alignment, but may be misguided about what The Agenda is or how to implement it, because the CEO has left too much room for ambiguity. Don't blame the company if you aren't communicating clearly or managing the outliers.

Just as often, a CEO struggling with misalignment is dealing with the ambition of the executive team. Here is an important thing to keep in mind if you are in this phase of your life cycle: If you are a CEO and you think people are out to get you, you're absolutely right. As Henry Kissinger once noted, "Even the paranoid have real enemies."

The CEO has been hired by the board either to fix something or to take the business somewhere it's never been. The board has a goal it believes is possible, but only achievable through a transition. The CEO's mandate is to implement that new direction—that "something completely different."

But most people on the executive committee don't actually want a transition. In fact, they are often incentivized against it. These people are smart, ambitious, successful, and good at their jobs—or at least, they are good at the narrow, currently defined versions of their jobs. Any transition poses a danger to them and their stability. People in these positions aren't keen to take risks that might jeopardize their success, particularly if they are happy where they are or don't agree that those risks are worth taking. It's very common for entrenched executives to greet a new CEO with a "wait and see" attitude: They are waiting to see whether these risky new ideas are worthwhile. They hunker down safely under the cover of the status quo, marking time until the CEO establishes himself or gets fired. This limits the actual momentum the CEO can generate, because it robs him of one of the key resources he needs to help with the required lifting: a unified and aligned ExCo.

Worse, many of the people on the executive committee will happily apply for the CEO position once it opens up (equipped with their myopic views of organizational success and their risk aversion). Some of them probably applied for the job the last time around and were passed over in favor of you—the person who is now asking them to take "unnecessary" risks. From their perspective, it seems best to do nothing because the sooner you fail, the sooner they can create new opportunities for themselves.

Willful misalignment, therefore, is generally an outcome of incongruent beliefs, which lead to opposing behaviors. The ambition of those on the executive committee motivates them to cling to their own beliefs and behaviors and actively oppose The Agenda. But they're smart. They don't want to get called out. So their opposition rarely comes in the form of direct confrontation. It tends to come in the form of tactical scapegoating or stalling. The CEO is likely to hear a lot of "yes" but see results that amount to a lot of "no." Meeting after meeting is filled with affirming head-nods, but no follow-up is forthcoming because those on the executive committee know they can get away with it. Why? Because, there is almost never an agreed-upon system of accountability.

Non-negotiable accountabilities to drive alignment

Non-negotiable accountabilities focus executive members efforts on activities that drive The Agenda. First, how are they expected to think about The Agenda? The answer you desire: *Your Agenda* is the *only* agenda. Second, how are they required to act? What does their complete engagement look like, behaviorally? This will require their undivided attention, as most organizations build metrics only around results, leaving tremendous opportunity for undisciplined behavior to compromise or complicate those results.

The goal at this phase of a CEO's life cycle is to spread his **conviction**—his deep belief in The Agenda—throughout the organization, in order to increase his **relevance** and his ability to accomplish that agenda. The goal is to get clear information via a second source, vetted with intuition that can be trusted to help discern the chicken from the feathers—in short, to remove the ambiguity.

The Agenda must be framed in such a way that the executive committee can understand it. And we're not just talking about clear language. We've seen CEOs give speeches and present PowerPoint slides and talk until they're blue in the face without achieving results. Everything has been on-message and everyone in the meeting seems to have a general understanding—but "general" understanding isn't good enough. General understanding still leaves people wondering, "What am I supposed to do? How do all those words apply to me?"

Because you are the CEO, everything you say is listened to. Unfortunately, it may be heard through any number of filters: *Do I need to do anything with this? Is he just talking or is this actually important? Will I ever hear any of this again? Will this hit my back pocket? Will I be held accountable for this?*

All this interference waters down your core message, creating the need for you to signpost non-negotiable accountabilities in these terms:

- What behaviors will or will not be acceptable?

- What thinking will or will not be tolerated?

- How will individual and collective success be measured and rewarded?

In order to achieve this, we recommend that a CEO spend some quality time with his team, discussing what's important to the ExCo members and what's important to the CEO. As commonalities emerge, you can draft these into a set of non-negotiable accountabilities that all agree to and accept. If there are items that aren't common but that you feel strongly about, include them also. This should not be a big list, but include four or five key themes such as:

- No surprises

- Deliver on all commitments

- Rigorous debate should occur in private and unity demonstrated in public,

- Etc.

Agree also on the appropriate consequences for breaches. Remember, these are **non-negotiable,** so any and all breaches should have agreed-upon consequences with teeth. The non-negotiable accountabilities become the measuring stick of performance, thus depersonalizing any consequences you must inflict when the inevitable politics and turf wars hit. This process will ensure that the individuals on your team don't feel singled out or unjustly dealt with when you need to correct foul play.

It always surprises us how much time the members of an ExCo spend together, but how little of it is dedicated to providing absolute clarity on these bedrock issues. Whether explicit or implicit, all CEOs have non-negotiables written on their hearts. Unfortunately few make them—or the consequences for breaching them—explicit, thus creating the need for mind reading on the part of their executives.

This simple but powerful exercise can rapidly align an ExCo in their thinking, acting, and delivery. It also has the added benefit of flushing out and exposing the misaligned.

This exercise and others like it promote understanding among the executive committee of how The Agenda affects them and their careers. It's not enough just to hear them say "yes." They have to generate measurable results that substantiate that "yes."

The way to ensure that your team is working toward The Agenda is to evaluate them and provide metrics for success based solely on progress toward it. If you reward them according to how many of your goals they achieve, then you unambiguously show them a way to succeed within the organization.

The alternative is to talk a good game about what you want the company to accomplish but then fail to make it explicitly clear that the team will be evaluated according to those accomplishments. If you do this, they will sit in your meetings, listen politely, smile, and then go about their business, doing exactly whatever it takes to be perceived as successful and compensated accordingly.

Once The Agenda is tied to metrics of thought and behavior, your people will have clarity about whether or not they are working toward the right goals and how they must go about accomplishing them. And once those metrics are tied to incentives, additional opportunities, or any other kind of reward, they will understand *why* they should work toward those goals.

When the members of your team are measuring their own success according to your mandate, and when you are rewarding them and compensating them on the same criteria, that is alignment.

As soon as the organization aligns with The Agenda, everything falls into place. People are either with the program or against it, because everyone knows what the program is. They are playing politics or playing to win—and they are playing to win together, instead of trying to win at one another's expense.

When executives are measured according to their adherence to The Agenda, you finally get clarity on the "chicken/feather" conundrum: You are able to ascertain what to trust.

What currencies does your enterprise use?

Every enterprise has its own "currencies" i.e., what the company and its culture value and reward. These are the things executives use as a standard of exchange to measure and trade power.

Title and salary are two obvious currencies indicating **formal power**, but they are not the only currencies. Others exist, and understanding them reveals a network of **informal power** that often paints a clearer picture of how the enterprise actually runs.

We deliberately use the word *currency*, as opposed to *culture*, because the word connotes two things: first, *power*, as in electric current; and second, that the power exists in the present moment i.e., it's current.

For example, some companies value tenure: The longer an employee has been around, the more knowledge and institutional wisdom he is presumed to have, so he is respected and valued for that. A person who can walk directly into the CEO's office without a scheduled appointment is presumed to have a lot of informal power.

Every organization has its own kinds of currencies that are considered valuable within the workplace, and they can take many forms: office location (city, building, floor, office size), geography (proximity to the power base, HQ vs. Gulag), budget, headcount, etc. This informal power is mutable—it can change with varying circumstances—but people always know what it is at any given time.

In a bear market, one of the currencies is the ability to retain or even add full-time employees to a department. Market downturns lead to hiring freezes and culling in response to shrinking budgets, so the executives who have a high headcount of FTEs and a large budget are the ones with the power—and everyone sees it. Conversely, during times of growth everyone has sufficient headcount, so the value of full-time employees as a form of currency goes down. During those times, the power may belong to the executives who own the clients or are closest to the revenue.

Relationships can also be a powerful form of currency. If an employee has a strong network, it can be leveraged to get things done. This can be a currency.

The actual currencies that are valued within a company vary, but what never varies is that the people who hold the most currency are also seen as the most powerful—often regardless of their title. We've seen plenty of capsized organizations in which the head of a certain function is more powerful than the CEO. This is important for any CEO to understand, but it's particularly important for a new CEO or one who is struggling to gain traction.

When the new CEO sets an agenda and rewards people for adherence to it, the CEO is making loyalty a currency. "Give me your loyalty," the CEO says, "and you will be rewarded with trust and responsibility in this organization. You will be compensated, promoted, and anointed."

Loyalty is the first currency

For a CEO navigating the first dilemma, *loyalty* is the first currency. Loyalty can and should be accelerated and engineered. You don't have a lot of time; you must get results. You need to show stakeholders you are on track. And to do this, you've got to win over some hearts and minds. You've got to get the executive committee collectively pulling in the same direction and at pace. If you can't create that momentum, your tenure as CEO is in jeopardy before it has even begun.

Here's an example of momentum generation from our consulting practice concerning a petrochemical firm making a bid to extend its international footprint. The story illustrates what we mean when we talk about creating essential momentum by establishing a single agenda.

***

The firm purchased a major asset from a global petrochemical giant. As part of the negotiations, the seller wanted a second asset included in the deal—an unloved, unwanted problem child that had not turned a profit in years. Rather than scupper the deal, the negotiating team accepted the terms. They knew the asset they really wanted would be hugely profitable from day one.

The unwanted business resided in a small European community that depended on the jobs it provided. Having always been a cash drain on the seller, and now in a down cycle forecast to last for another four years, they were very pleased to get rid of it.

The employees' loyalty extended no further than their next paycheck, and a sense of entitlement had taken hold of the workforce. Investment in the division had always been scarce, and the new owners found themselves burdened with an unsafe, thirty-year-old petrochemical facility and potential PR disaster. The prevailing employee mantra came as a shock to the new owners: "If you want to survive at this company, check your brain at the gate."

We were recommended to the newly appointed CEO. After a series of intense and pointed conversations with him, it was clear he was facing Dilemma One. He needed to establish his agenda rapidly in order to mitigate the personal and corporate risk of the UXB he had been handed. We agreed to "look under the hood" of this business in order to determine the size of the challenge. Here's what we found:

Core issues

1   **A loser mentality and no pride among employees.** The place looked like a teenager's bedroom, with piles of stuff lying around and every surface in need of cleaning or painting. The general attitude was akin to that of a night watchman: "I am here to watch but not to participate." Evidence of past neglect showed on every face, in every attitude, and in every area.

2　**Consequences of the cyclical nature of the industry.** How do you make money from an asset that has not turned a profit in years—during a down cycle? Petrochemical plants are like cars: They run best when you drive them frequently on the open road. This asset had been sitting in the garage for a while, and it was in bad shape.

3　**Lack of respect for management.** The average tenure for non-executives was twenty-one years; in contrast, average tenure for executives was eighteen months. This company was clearly viewed by executives as a short-term career pit stop that might not even show up on their resumes. As a result, they were looking to "do no harm" or—at best—attempt an experimental "quick fix" and move on before it caught up to them. Every twelve to eighteen months, some new hotshot would come in and change everything ... which, in reality, meant that nothing ever changed. The real power remained in the hands of the employees, not the executives.

4　**Lack of employee engagement.** Under the circumstances mapped out above, it was not surprising that the employees were just there to collect paychecks. The previous owners' strategy of parachuting in a succession of executives to "run the facility" had put a damper on upward mobility within the workforce, leaving them profoundly unmotivated. Literally, an employee had to wait for the guy above him to retire or die to secure a promotion.

5　**Constrained economics.** Because of the fiscal state of the company, the new owner was willing to allocate only two resources to the project—the CEO and an experienced COO. The odds were definitely not in their favor: 2,500 employees to two executives. Add to that an extremely meager budget.

Core assets

1 **A highly trained workforce.** Although the workforce was unengaged, they were highly trained and had decades of experience at safely running this asset on a shoestring. In fact, what they had done to date in spite of their constraints was admirable.

2 **Employees who needed their jobs.** Despite their lack of cooperation and entitled behavior, every employee understood the reality of his situation: If he were to lose his job, it would be difficult or even impossible to find another one within the small community.

3 **Buy-sell capabilities.** The new owner was more than just an operator/producer; it had trading capabilities within the group that could possibly be leveraged.

4 **Expectation that the new owner would close the plant.** When the two-for-one deal was made public, the pundits and public alike expected that the new owner would close the facility as soon as legally possible.

5 **No blame for failure.** As long as there were no catastrophes or fatalities, the new CEO really could not be blamed for failing where so many others had also failed.

So … what do you do with an unloved child? In short, give it some love by being clear about what you expect, reward positive behavior, and allow it to earn respect. Here's the twelve-month plan that was implemented.

1   **Paint for Pride.** Everyone in the business was required to come in for a full weekend to clean and paint the entire site. Despite some initial grumblings, people got into the spirit of the event. (It helped that food and light entertainment were provided.) A total of $100,000 was invested (most of which was spent on paint). The impact on employee pride was amazing! The place looked beautiful and everyone wanted to keep it that way. So much so that the spruce-up became a yearly tradition involving whole families.

2   **Not the usual town hall meetings.** Many of those entrenched in the middle of the organization were obstructionists. To ameliorate this, all employees were invited in groups of a hundred to a series of "meet the new owners" sessions. Although the new owners had not yet determined whether or not they would keep the new asset, they spoke honestly to each small group, defusing fear and anger and engendering a positive, hopeful environment.

3   **An opportunity to set The Agenda.** Two months after the above meetings took place, another round of meetings was held. First, the overall strategy was shared with the entire business: You make as much product as you safely can and we will sell it. Then, in small groups, people were encouraged to share their ideas about how success could be accelerated,

and what might potentially block it. The results were shared with all employees, and key influencers were identified to help resolve the blockages.

The above steps created a sense of clarity—a sense that *these guys are different; they listen, engage, give clear direction, and also really seem to care.* With the beginnings of trust established, each individual and working group in the organization was given an opportunity to answer the question "What have you always wanted to do that would accelerate performance, but felt you couldn't?" This provoked a veritable tsunami of pent-up innovation! Over 90 percent of the employees' suggestions were implemented—and ironically, 95 percent within their own working groups. All along they'd had the answers, but no hope.

So what about the dysfunctional ExCo? In short, the kids were excused and the adults invited to the party. Within a year, all appointments to the new ExCo were internal—those who had been coached and earned the right to be there as a result of their contributions and their ability to lead others.

More and more employees came to see that career progression was possible. Over the next few years, many of these leaders went on to senior roles elsewhere in the new owners' group of companies.

The results

1   In a down market and for over a decade, hundreds of millions in losses were turned into hundreds of millions in profit. Surprisingly to everyone, including the new owners, a $50

million per annum loss was reversed into a $50 million gain within the first eighteen months of trading.

2   The facility continually broke thirty-year production records.

3   The company maintained an exemplary safety record, with no accidents or fatalities.

4   The executives are now respected and the workforce remains engaged.

Total investment was a bit of paint, our fees, and a lot of time spent aligning the organization.

***

It always amazes us what real alignment brings to a business, and though much has been written about *what* to do, too few businesses are truly aligned. Understanding *how* to engineer alignment is not as easy as it seems on paper, and far more expansive than a few well-rehearsed talking points. Knowing precisely how to bring about the necessary alignment, gives businesses the confidence and flexibility to cater for the organizational currencies and cultures at play. For most of us we learned to ride a bicycle when we were young, probably using training wheels or a loved ones steadying hand. Can you remember the exhilarating feeling of the first time you rode unassisted? Up until that point it was all theory, you knew *what* to do but had not yet benefitted from the experience of *how* to do it. Only after several scraped knees and bruised elbows did you master the basics of how to ride and that is when it got really fun. Soon you became more advanced, jumping everything in sight and venturing onto more challenging terrain. It probably became your main mode of transportation and usually involved fun, freedom, and friends—in time you became very experienced at riding all kinds of vehicles with two wheels. Even though some of us have never stopped riding, and consider ourselves to be very competent, others have developed their know-how into an art form. Every year in a virtually unknown part of the United States, Virgin Utah, is host to the world's toughest invitation-only free ride event—The Red Bull Rampage. Virgin's uniquely demanding terrain provides the backdrop for one of the toughest and most intense events in the sport of free ride mountain bike racing. It is hard to imagine that each of the participants at some point started riding like you and I. They took their understanding of how to ride and have pushed themselves and their peers and created an art form that is jaw dropping to behold. Some CEOs we meet still have their metaphorical training wheels on and though they know what to do, they get stuck when trying to align their team and organization because they lack experience and the proper know how. The power of alignment resides in the vast understanding of how, not an intellectually stimulating agreement of what needs to be done. As alignment increases, it strengthens individual and collective loyalty.

Creating a currency of loyalty is the cornerstone to building sustainable momentum and ensuring that you deliver on your mandate. Rewarding adherence to The Agenda ensures that people are focused on what you want. It gets them engaged in the conversations you need them to have, and it gets them leading on your behalf. Loyalty starts with belief in the CEO and his direction, then transitions to the actual agreed-upon outcomes, allowing for healthy challenge and vetting instead of blind devotion to an individual.

Another useful but simple exercise to undertake at this point is to list each of your executive members and rate them as Positive (+),

Neutral (0), or Negative (–) toward you and The Agenda. Observe them over a few weeks to confirm or change your intuition. In attempting to determine where to invest their scarce time, most CEOs attempt to quiet the squeaky wheel or turn the negative people into positives. This is, in our assessment, a tactical error, as you waste so much time trying to persuade the negative ones that you run the risk of losing the positives and neutrals. A more effective approach is to focus your energy on the positives (especially those with a lot of currency), who in turn can help you influence the neutrals. This creates a critical mass of momentum that forces the negatives to make a choice: join the party or be left out in the cold. Each of them will either get on board or leave, and you will have solidified critical resources.

Your metrics will begin to reveal the people who are most loyal to The Agenda, and you will earmark these people and pull them closer. Everyone in the organization will understand what that means: Loyalty is now the prime currency. Your actions will tell people, clearly and without any ambiguity, "I don't care how long you've been here, how much revenue you drive, or how important you think your client relationships are to this business. Competency is a commodity anyone can acquire. What matters most is loyalty, which is manifested through engagement." Anyone who wants to succeed in your company now has a clear path to success: alignment with The Agenda.

One way to send a message to your company about the value of loyalty is to reward it. Reinforce the desired behavior with public accolades, highlighting examples of the desired behavior. Remove access limitations, heighten transparency, purposefully engineer greater visibility to the board, include them on pre-meets, and seek their input on critical decisions.

Establishing non-negotiable accountabilities will create a level of transparency across the ExCo, focusing all executive efforts on priorities that drive The Agenda. This clarity will either accelerate alignment or lack thereof as there will be nowhere to hide, the bottom line- no passengers only crew members.

In a desperate, last-ditch effort to save face, nine out of ten misaligned ExCo members will self-select and "vote with their feet." They will announce their resignations. Despite the exciting future you have set forth, and "after great consideration," they will decide to pursue other opportunities outside of the organization.

The benefit to the employer of a specific ExCo member's resignation is the elimination of lengthy negotiations, disruption to team momentum, and inappropriate corporate expenditure. All of this is a result of active or passive resistance to alignment, which is *not* an enterprise responsibility.

The one out of ten misaligned executives who are *not* inclined to move on may need to be removed. Doing so certainly sends a clear signal, and removing someone significant—someone with a lot of currency within the organization who isn't getting on board with The Agenda—is necessary to unite the team that remains. It sends a wake-up call to the entire operation, a declaration that you mean business and everyone needs to pay attention—understanding The Agenda and non-negotiables that are now in place.

The level of visibility involved in the firing depends on how much attention you want your decision to get. A highly visible removal will certainly shake up an executive committee that is entrenched in a culture of foot-dragging, hunkering down, and trying to protect its own siloed interests. Very few actions a new CEO can take will yield such beneficial and immediate results. The person under fire probably has a lot of currency within the company, and it has made him confident enough to stand (actively or passively) in opposition to your success. This person will hinder you and destroy critical team momentum because he believes he is bigger and more important than The Agenda. Removing this person states loudly and clearly to everyone that no one is untouchable. The Agenda is more important than any single personality. The follow-up action is to replace that counterproductive team member with someone aligned, loyal, and highly competent who will accelerate momentum.

In our experience, the less seasoned CEO picks competence over loyalty every time, as they fear the risks of making the big calls alone. Few sporting coaches have the resolve to bench their franchise player during their first year on the job. And let's be honest, the competent ones are usually the stars; they score the points you will be judged on. We challenge you to rethink this paradigm.

CEOs with more seasoning inherently know that at this point in their life cycle, momentum is crucial. As a result, they know they must choose loyalty first and competence second. To do otherwise would require the expenditure of too much precious time and emotional energy on distracting power struggles and compromises, pandering and placating to one player while disenfranchising the rest of the ExCo, who may not be able to get enough quality airtime on their most pressing issues.

We can hear you objecting: "But that means I might be carrying less competent team members—and that will signal that I'm creating the wrong culture—or worse." Remember this is a two-step dance. The issue, for now, is to create enough momentum that you will eventually be able to establish *your* team and *your* culture. You can only do that via loyalty and alignment, not mere competence. If you choose wisely at this point, you will leverage the newly instilled currency of loyalty even above personalities or competence. Knowing that you have given the misaligned ample opportunity to align will give you—and most importantly, your ExCo—peace of mind. They will see that you are clear, fair, and uncompromising in your expectations.

What we are really saying is that we know these calls can be tough, but if your actions are clear and decisive, the entire organization will see the need for key departures.

The momentum created by the strategy of choosing *loyalty first* will only last for a season, but that is definitely long enough to backfill short-term competency gaps that might emerge and establish the foundation of an even stronger currency of loyalty and competence. It is a scary jump to make, but a necessary one.

As a result of these actions, everyone will understand that loyalty is a highly valued currency—that The Agenda is more important than any single personality—and that presents each person with a choice: Get on board with The Agenda or look for opportunities elsewhere.

In our experience, the removal of a misaligned executive has never been damaging to the enterprise—although the *how* is critical, and self-selection is the most common result. As we noted above, 90 percent of the misaligned choose to move on. Attempting to keep the misaligned is like putting one foot on the brake and the other on the gas: It burns a lot of energy and gets you nowhere. Once you have the courage to let the blockage clear itself (and help in the few cases in which that is necessary), a collective sigh will arise from the remaining team and you will wonder why it took you so long to act.

No action other than letting people leave—or firing them if necessary—accelerates the alignment of the executive committee faster or makes it more obvious who is in and who is out.

The rest of the executive committee knew that the misaligned person was blocking your success and keeping the company from beginning its transition. Removing him tells your team that you are willing to do what it takes to move forward, and it signals hope and opportunity for everyone who is ready to get on board. It reaffirms that you mean business, and that the company for which they work has a clear direction and a courageous leader at the helm.

When the executive committee understands The Agenda and how it affects them—that it is the path to reward, and their refusal to collectively pursue that path will not be accepted—this gives you exactly what you need: a surge of momentum and a loyal team that is ready to get to work. In a word, it gives you, the CEO, *relevance*.

Indicators that you are stuck in Dilemma One

- Multiple competing agendas that are power-driven, not purpose-driven

- A politically charged environment in which there is a lot of babysitting

- Behavior accountabilities are inconsistent or ignored—especially for the favorites
- Core decisions are made by the inner circle only—just the trusted few
- Visible misalignment: you hear "yes" but see a whole lot of "no"
- Incessant power struggles: the tail wagging the dog
- Triangulation of data for reasons of trust not verification
- Validation from *in*-the-business execution, not aligned results
- Overpopulation of B and C players: few resources to delegate to
- Focus is on *who*, not *what*, with an emphasis on placing blame
- Competence is valued over alignment or loyalty

Indicators that you have mastered Dilemma One

- There is only one agenda: Your Agenda
- Non-negotiables are clear and adhered to
- Politics have been noted and minimized
- Trustworthy executives make for trustworthy data
- Rewards and consequences are aligned to The Agenda
- You have a loyal and engaged ExCo to whom you feel confident delegating
- Clarity has removed confusion and hesitation from B and C players

- There is engagement beyond the inner circle to the broader executive

- The focus is on the *what* not the *who*, on solutions rather than personalities

- Your role as CEO is undisputed

3

The second dilemma

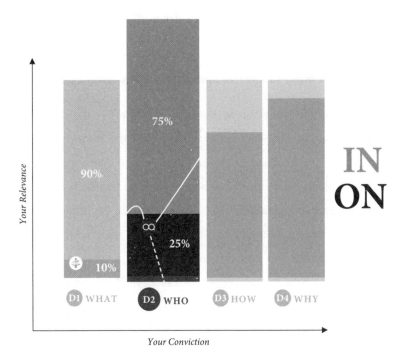

The previous dilemma addressed Phase One of the CEO life cycle and was about validating what you have inherited—the people, the corporate culture, and so on—as it relates to your mandate. The next dilemma, which arises in Phase Two, is about transitioning from an inherited ExCo to *your* handpicked ExCo—and then mobilizing them to fulfill your mandate.

Your inherited ExCo was probably a mixed bag; ranging from willfully misaligned to aligned and actively pursuing The Agenda, from openly disloyal adversaries to trusted lieutenants, and from incompetent for today's needs to very able for tomorrow's challenges. In Dilemma One you will have dealt with misalignment, disloyalty, and incompetence—in short, those who won't make the journey. You are now left with a group of aligned and loyal executives with varying degrees of competence to make the journey ahead. This brings us to the second CEO dilemma:

You know today's executive cannot deliver tomorrow's results.

Initiating the transition to the ultimate "who" is the next step toward ensuring that you can eventually shift the balance of your work from *in* the business to *on* the business. With your head buried in day-to-day operations and picking up the slack of lower-functioning team members, you can never hope to progress to a point of sustained momentum. You will remain stuck with as many spinning plates as you yourself can spin.

After successful completion of your tasks in Phase One, you are in a position of increased relevance and conviction. The politics at the top have been minimized and the message of *what* you intend the ExCo and broader organization to focus on is crystal clear. This has created a positive forward momentum that can be seen, and most important, felt. This is the time to step up and be intentional about selecting and deploying *your* ExCo so that they are capable of getting you through the next phase of your journey.

A word of caution: Too many CEOs who successfully navigate Phase One mistake their newfound momentum and the absence of noise that results from clear direction and initial alignment as a "job done," when in fact the job has only just begun. At first, the contents of this chapter may seem overly simplistic and perhaps a bit naïve. But in the real world, most CEOs fail to get the selection of their ExCo right. Many settle for what they've inherited, with few substantive changes. They continue to spin the plates.

CEOs who do not make executive selection a priority spend most of their time working *around* certain ExCo members rather than working *through* them. This is a "do not pass go" moment. It is a make-or-break moment. It is so important that we have devoted the majority of this chapter to the mechanics of selecting *your* ExCo.

If you are in any doubt about those you work around, they are the ones you tell your PA to put off until next week or month. You know the ones we mean. The ones who inspire eye rolls or even audible groans from their fellow executives every time they open their mouths. They tend to be functional experts on a mission to protect the world from momentum, creativity, or commercial viability. It's as if they only know one tune: "Chopsticks."

Perhaps you find yourself scheduling a meeting when you know they are unavailable so you can actually get something done. You know they won't add enterprise value, let alone build a following. The question is "why do you and others continue to work around these people?" Because you certainly aren't working with or through them! Let's be clear, it's not that these people are incompetent; in fact, the opposite is probably the case. It is just that they are so narrow in their focus and expertise that you can only use them surgically.

The antithesis is the person you wish you could clone: the one you choose to work through! He has both functional and enterprise-wide abilities, if you could only have more like him.

***

Toward the end of his career, the legendary nineteenth-century industrialist and philanthropist Andrew Carnegie accurately, if modestly, described himself as "a man who knew how to enlist in his service better men than himself." Carnegie is an icon within modern business literature, and rightly so. Born poor in Scotland, he started working as a telegrapher when just a teen and ultimately went on to found the great Carnegie Steel conglomerate. He is remembered today for the size and success of his company, as well as the breadth of his charitable giving, which focused on the creation of numerous public libraries, New York's Carnegie Hall, and the Peace Palace in The Hague. He even commissioned Napoleon Hill to interview other successful men and write one of the most influential business books of all time, *Think and Grow Rich*.

Less attention has been paid to the individuals Carnegie chose as partners and members of his trusted management team—but in a book largely about identifying and leveraging the capability of top talent, we thought it relevant to spend a bit of time on the key individuals who made up Carnegie's inner circle.

While puff pieces about Carnegie suggest that as many as fifty men worked together to lead his enterprise, in point of fact, a mere handful of individuals bore the bulk of the responsibilities. Each is legendary today, inside and outside manufacturing circles, in large measure because of the role he played alongside Carnegie and what they were able to accomplish together.

Long before American investors were exhorted to "Talk to Chuck," the original Charles Schwab became known for his unique ability to bring together disparate forces and help them find common ground. Recognizing Schwab's gift for making labor peace through diplomacy rather than force, Carnegie appointed him president of Carnegie Steel Company at the tender age of thirty-five, at a then-unimaginable salary of $1 million per year.

Henry Clay Frick, best known today for the eponymous art gallery in his former Fifth Avenue mansion, also started early. Frick had honed his skills in sales, customer service, and bookkeeping before he was out of his teens. While still in his early twenties, he recognized the importance of the raw material coke to the process of making steel and formed a company to produce the substance in large quantities. The panic of 1873 nearly cost him his company, but he bought out his partner's shares and went on to sell a sizable percentage of the firm to Andrew Carnegie. Frick brought his acumen for numbers into Carnegie's employ and became the Chairman of Carnegie Steel Corporation—playing a vital role in the continuing growth of the company.

Henry Phipps, neither as well known nor as controversial as Schwab and Frick, was a boyhood friend of Carnegie's who began as a bookkeeper and ended up a financier for Carnegie Steel Corporation and the company's second-largest shareholder. Unlike most of the robber barons of the era, Phipps possessed a social conscience and devoted himself to philanthropic causes. Notably, he was involved in the development of high-quality, low-income housing.

Carnegie's cousin, George Lauder Jr., grew up alongside him in Scotland and graduated from Glasgow University with a degree in mechanical engineering. Once his company was thriving, Carnegie wrote to Lauder in Scotland and invited him to come and join the management team. Wisely, Lauder accepted the invitation and became Carnegie's closest confidant and advisor; he is credited with various industrial innovations that took the company to even greater heights.

Build or buy? Most enterprises face this decision at various points in their development. For Carnegie Steel, the question was whether to buy into an existing pig-iron factory or instead to invest in the creation of a more modern facility. Under the direction of Carnegie's brother Thomas, Carnegie Steel built its own pig-iron facility, designed to run hotter and more efficiently than any before it. Thomas was widely admired for his conservative approach and proved to be an astute operator.

Andrew Carnegie tended to select self-made men who had worked their way up from the bottom, often occupying several different positions in the company as they rose through the ranks. He believed in trial by fire, confronting promising employees with challenges and then promoting or demoting them based on how they managed these situations. This method tended to produce people practiced in dealing with nearly every aspect of a business—from raw materials to distribution. Thus, even though each member of his team had his own particular area of expertise, they all had the background necessary to deal with the company in its totality.

That didn't necessarily mean that they always agreed. Frick, for example, was notorious for his tough stance on labor negotiations, whereas Henry Phipps (and Carnegie himself) had positioned themselves as more even-handed. This was where a diplomatic type like Charles Schwab was invaluable. He could devise solutions that pleased both parties while still increasing productivity in the Carnegie steel mills.

At one time or another, all of these men had these types of ideological clashes over how to manage the myriad challenges all businesses face. To be successful, they learned to set aside their individual preferences and consider a third option—a collaborative approach developed in concert with the other team members. All members of his tight-knit inner circle had to be capable of making enterprise-wide decisions.

That is just one example of the ways in which Carnegie's handpicked team propelled his company to greater and greater heights. Schwab was tasked with managing labor relations, while Frick oversaw raw materials. Lauder was in charge of technological innovations, while Phipps kept a grip on the financial reins. Thomas Carnegie brought to the party his own technical wizardry and openness to innovation. Andrew Carnegie's talents were his vision, organization, and willingness to take risks. But just as important as any of those was his gift for identifying, recruiting, and retaining highly talented individuals vital to the growth of the company.

What does *your* team look like? Would it pass a Carnegie litmus test? Will you, like Carnegie before you, be remembered as one "who knew how to enlist in his service better men (and women) than himself"?

***

In our experience, getting ExCo selection right kills any remaining politics, weeds out the myopic, and sets the tone of your tenure, enabling you to infuse the entire organization with excellence.

Imagine a situation in which your ExCo members were capable of doing one another's jobs as well as yours. What if their direct reports could do the same for their bosses? Is this a scary thought or an exhilarating one?

What if these important groups of leaders intuitively knew *what* needed to be done and *how* to best get it done—for individuals, teams, and the organization as a whole? It may sound impossible, but it's not. We have played an active part in making this a reality for countless CEOs and their organizations.

Think of the capacity that could be generated and the bench strength of talent you could have at your disposal. You could win in any market you chose to conquer.

You hold the power

In defeat and out of necessity, you begin to have the real conversations and make the real decisions outside the formal structure. This is OK—or shall we say *was* OK—for a while. Though you did not initially choose your senior team or establish your inherited culture, now you must. The honeymoon is over. This state of affairs cannot be allowed to become the new normal or it will stunt any future growth of the enterprise and of you as CEO. You have the power to reshape the ExCo, and now is the time to exercise it.

We recognize this can be a difficult time for you, as your ExCo has worked hard to get you and the organization on the right trajectory. They have demonstrated both alignment to The Agenda and loyalty to you. They may even feel they have earned their seat at the table.

You may also feel a desire to reward their effort or to fulfill a promise you should not have made. Making additional changes can feel and be seen as disloyal—yet, in your heart you know your intuition is right. Not everyone will be competent enough to make the entire journey, at least in his current role. We recommend utilizing the power of Predictive Analytics to discover previously undetected executive patterns using data and algorithms, this type of analysis highlights your "A players" and those capable of making the entire journey. Your decisions must be grounded in current and future competence, as you cannot afford the drag that a less competent member will have on your ExCo.

ExCo bench strength

Your ultimate aim is to have every member of your executive loyal and competent for now and in the future. Since you have removed the incompetent and misaligned and built strong foundations of loyalty, you are now left with only a competence issue. The essential task now is to ensure that you have the highest caliber of executive talent available: guaranteeing that ALL are A players. We refer to this as an ExCo's "bench strength"—the readiness of potential successors to move into key positions as you move through the critical transition process.

As you are aware, there is a significant difference between those who are *incompetent* and those who are *less competent*. The less competent are not able to generate the required capacity lift, so they will need to be layered; buffered with more competent people at

Levels 1 and 2. Here is a good test to determine the capacity in your current ExCo composition.

If you were to promote each person or move him sideways tomorrow, what would be the consequences? If the answer about any given person is that the consequences would be dire for the enterprise, you have the wrong person. He is either too much of a specialist or too important in his current role to be moved. Either of these situations reveals a significant competency problem that will require you to reach down continually—to spend time *in* the business.

In either case, the person probably needs to be layered, as capacity generation at this juncture in your life cycle becomes essential. The real question becomes who will make the cut and what do you do with those who don't?

IQ, EQ, and OQ

In order to assist you further in your quest for a competent and loyal ExCo, we would like to introduce you to a rubric we call OQ— Organizational Quotient. You are no doubt familiar with Intelligence Quotient (IQ) and Emotional Quotient (EQ). You probably have an above-average score on both of these measures of intelligence—but we all know reports, colleagues, and competitors who have higher scores. Why were you selected as CEO over these capable and bright individuals? Luck, timing, hard work, and connections may have played a part—but was there perhaps something more fundamental—and that something was probably OQ. CEOs we work with find OQ an extremely useful criterion when selecting and empowering their ExCo.

We have often heard a chairman describe his CEO by saying, "He just *gets it.*" We hear CEOs describe their most valued executives the same way. When pressed further, they usually struggle to pinpoint what "it" is. True, those we value most do "get it." They don't have to be told what to do, nor do they need to be babysat or cleaned up after. They constantly deliver the right results in the right way while managing expectations. There are no unpleasant surprises. They are a pleasure to work with; we are proud to be associated with them, and ultimately we legitimize their efforts and give them near unlimited access.

What quality do they have that allows them to "get it"? We maintain that it isn't IQ or EQ, but OQ; the ability to discern clearly *what* needs to be done and the *know-how* to get it delivered in the right way for you, for their team, and for the organization. Individuals with a high OQ are your superstars, your franchise players, your *A players*. Here's the model:

Executives' lives are dominated by achieving *results*, building and defending personal and team brand and *reputation*, and *aligning* with what they believe needs to be done so they can acquire the *power* necessary to defend and grow their kingdoms. The school of hard knocks, numerous scars, and time on the battlefield have also taught seasoned executives the hierarchal relationship among these factors. This is what matters in their world.

When you were appointed CEO, your board, whether consciously or not, was judging you through the lenses of consistent undisputed *results*, a *reputation* that precedes your physical presence and *aligns* with their values and style, and their faith that you would build the *power* and influence necessary to deliver the mandate they have entrusted you with. Should it be any different for your ExCo appointments at this stage?

Metaphorically speaking, you have thus far been dating the ExCo, and now you are faced with the greater commitment of marriage. Whom will you choose? No longer will the positions be held over; they will intentionally be filled, either by the people who now hold them or by new people. As in marriage, your choice reflects who you are and what you stand for, and you intend to get it right.

Two internal drivers influence decision-making: attraction and proximity. These drivers stand like pillars through the OQ model, so bringing them to the forefront should prove helpful. As senior leaders, we develop a sixth sense about people and whether accurate or not, first impressions often stick. Attraction is immediate, and it is based on "like liking like." Attraction is answered by the question "Do I want to work with you?" Proximity, on the other hand, is earned over time and based on symbiotic fit with those we trust. It answers the question, "Do I *want* you close to me?" In your selection process, you need to be able to answer both of these questions in the affirmative.

***

Often when market opportunity presents itself, your time for preparation has passed. To say that the heat was on would have been the understatement of the century for this emerging market insurance provider. The health insurance market was practically on fire, and as one of the largest insurers in the region, the provider staged an incredibly successful IPO, resulting in a capital raise of $2 billion US for a minority share of the company. The goal—to organically become number one in their region.

The CEO admitted to us that he had overstretched himself, his team, and the business to get to where they were. Though he had been part of the organization for several years, previously serving as its finance director, he was new to the commander-in-chief role. He was also years younger than his colleagues. The strain of the last few years' efforts on systems and people was palpable, yet with the fresh injection of capital and a market ripe for harvest, expectations and scrutiny were stratospheric.

Feeling the pressure, the board recommended he get outside help. After a thorough review, it became very clear that the main challenge was a talent problem. The business had advanced so quickly to number three that its management had been put in place by what could best be described as "battlefield appointments"— whoever was available got the job.

Though his executive was aligned and loyal, most of them relied on their tenure and titles to get stuff done. The results of the review did not look good. In fact, only two of his six-member ExCo were deemed capable of making the journey in their current roles, and he was one of the two.

While many CEOs encounter this Dilemma Two problem, it was particularly poignant for two reasons: First, he operated in a relationship-driven culture in which loyalty was the prime currency and reward mechanism. Second, as in many emerging markets, the talent needed was very difficult to attract to the region. The real challenge became how to move forward without hindering the existing team from doing what they do best (working *in* the business) while simultaneously bringing on a more senior team capable of taking the business to number one and beyond.

We counseled the CEO, stressing that the business was at a critical, pivotal point. If he closed the talent gap, he could be number one. But if he chose to ignore the issue of ExCo competency, he would remain stuck... or worse, burn out trying to plug the competency gaps in his executive. It was clear *what* needed to be done, but in order to pull it off without compromising his current operation, he was relying on us to show him *how*. Once we worked through the *how*, he opted to close the gap, and we helped him choose the right players and ensure that they would be successful, individually and collectively. The plan looked like this:

1 Engage the board for assistance, especially chairman contacts.

2 Set expectations and stabilize the current ExCo.

3 Coach the head of sales (the other keeper) to become CCO.

4   Since operations was most at risk, immediately hire a new
    COO with potential to replace the CEO.

5   Since the CFO was acting as a financial controller, within six
    months hire a new CFO with enterprise-wide insight and
    potential to replace the CEO. Within the next six months,
    move customer relations and product development under his
    portfolio, ideally retaining current heads.

6   Since HR was the weakest function, hire the best functional
    expert possible. The CEO and ExCo would be responsible for
    talent acquisition and the culture.

7   Since the CEO was spending the majority of his time plugging
    competency gaps *in* the business, shift to 75 percent working
    on the business and increase external profile.

8   Coach past and future executives to ensure successful
    retention, acquisition, and monetization.

It took six months to establish the new ExCo, but after that it took only a short time to achieve the desired results. A year into the transition from being stuck *in* the business the CEO asked, "So what does a CEO really do?" He had never known the full capacity of his role or his organization. Once he could invest 75 percent of his time focusing *on* the business, these were the results.

–   All of the previous ExCo (except HR, an unregrettable loss)
    were retained during the transition and beyond.

–   Within two years, the business became number one across the
    region in profit. The following year and every year since, the
    business has been number one in profit, revenue, and market share.

–   The company has been recognized with multiple awards: Most Admired Company in the Region, Employer of Choice, Best Insurance Company of the Year, CEO of the Year, etc.

Finding talent is no longer a problem for this business, as it has become a regional talent magnet and a net exporter of innovation and people. The moral of the story is this: The best *insurance* against Dilemma Two is bringing the right people onto the team.

Delivering to The agenda

The first essential principle of OQ starts at the bottom left side of the pyramid and counsels all ExCo members to develop the discipline to consistently *look up* in order to deliver The Agenda. If they are unaware of how your efforts support The Agenda, it will be impossible for them to understand how the results you pursue actually matter. Once they learn to look up, alignment to the power base occurs. They begin to understand your deliverables by looking deeper into the organizational needs as they relate to your mandate.

It amazes us how often executives get this wrong. Their mindset says, "If I focus down into my silo and execute well, it will be noticed by my colleagues and the organization, or the CEO will look after me." This B-player mentality causes frustration when the goal posts move and no one tells them, or worse, they deliver a thing of beauty that no one wants or needs. An A player doesn't need to be told; he is organizationally aware because he is constantly looking up and calibrating. Looking up should not be confused with its political counterfeit—*managing up*. B players manage up while A players look up and deliver.

The discipline of looking up is necessary for any executive—including you. As CEO, you live in a world of ambiguity, where boundaries are often unclear and discernment is constantly required. CEOs get wiped out every day because they themselves fail to *look up* to see what the board requires or *look out* to see fundamental changes in key stakeholder sentiment. We have witnessed first-hand the frustration that chairmen and their boards can feel when their CEOs fail to read their implied signals of discontent. Unseasoned CEOs often adopt an openly defensive strategy or shrug off these attempts to steer them, instead of discerning what is behind these signals. The minute they leave the room, comments like, "He just doesn't get it" or "I think we have a problem" begin to be heard. The unspoken message is that if the chairman or the board have to be explicit with their CEO, they are doing his job for him—which may very well mean he is the wrong guy.

The most common things we see CEOs defend to their boards are pace (too slow or too fast), direction, budget, approach, and talent. The simple mistake is to *defend* rather than push for clarity. The breadcrumb of a complaint tossed by the board or chairman rarely encompasses the real issue. It is often just a message that something bigger needs fixing. Without probing, you will never be able to understand and address the real concerns.

Some CEOs feel they need to show strength and control, so they sell harder and double down, completely misreading the situation. When your relationship with the board and/or chairman begins to move from informal to formal, placing you at a greater distance, you may be at a dangerous pivot point in your career.

Once the board has to become explicit with you, you quickly become the wrong guy. The logic is this: *If we, the board, are doing your job for you, whose job are you doing?* At that point, emotions are running strong and you run the risk of losing perspective.

Bottom line: Rather than leaping to defend your choices—in hopes of appearing strong and decisive—we suggest you probe for greater clarity first.

Except in cases of pure hubris, the erosion of confidence in a CEO generally happens because he has failed to transition from working *in* the business to working *on* the business. This, as we've explained, is a result of having the wrong team in place and therefore continually having to reach down to do direct reports' jobs for them. The time-consuming activity of working intently *in* the business is bound to be observed by the board and can be emotionally very rewarding for some CEOs, as it makes them feel needed and creates a sense of dependency. But at this point in your life cycle, it is like crossing the road while looking down at your phone, thus overlooking the oncoming vehicle until the moment of impact.

In an effort to further clarify this extremely important concern, let's apply the principles of OQ to your ExCo. As you will see, the principles apply equally, whether you are looking up for alignment or down for mobilization and results.

The base: Results

Any ExCo member, or potential one, wants to put the best possible shine on his results—that's just human nature. But results must speak for themselves, without a spit-shine. You must be able to discern fact from fiction, the chicken from the feathers.

Of the four OQ keys, this is perhaps the easiest to measure, but it is nonetheless challenging because many executives confuse superb execution with aligned results. Results and execution are *not* the same thing: No matter how flawless the execution, it can deliver the wrong results—doing a great job building a thing of beauty that no one wants or needs. When this happens, it is because the executive has completely failed to look up and outside of his silo to align his efforts with the overall value of the organization and The Agenda.

Let's be clear: Looking up is a discipline anyone can master. Don't over-complicate it—just do it.

Delivering incorrect results is actually worse than non-delivery, because it is very difficult to unwind. The executive believes he was doing what was right for the business and passively holds onto this belief while throwing blame in everyone else's direction. The outcome is a visible misalignment with The Agenda and a need to save face with the team. Whether the executive's intentions were honorable or not, you can't ignore the need to call out misaligned execution and discipline the foolish.

For an exemplar of someone who did just that—that is, someone who produced results worth talking about, who never displayed an inflated sense of his own worth, and who never accused others for his failures—we can turn to the late Sir Donald Bradman, aka "The Don."

Many sports historians today regard Bradman as the greatest sportsman who ever lived—in all senses of the term. His good sportsmanship and civility in cricket stood out even in a sport uniquely noted for its emphasis on those qualities (it is not unheard-of for batsmen to "walk" if they believe themselves to be out, even if the umpire has not called them out).

Bradman's achievements on the field from 1927 to 1949 are legendary. His 99.94 career batting average is often cited as the greatest achievement in the global history of sports. An equivalent achievement in baseball would be a lifetime batting average of 0.392 (the great Ty Cobb only batted 0.366). An NBA player would need to achieve a career average of forty-three points per game in order to have an equivalent impact on basketball (Michael Jordan's average was 30.1). Bradman's face graced an Australian postage stamp during his lifetime—an unusual honor in any country—and a commemorative 20-cent coin after his death. Nelson Mandela is said to have asked, upon his release after twenty-seven years of imprisonment, "Is Sir Donald Bradman still alive?"[1]

His sportsmanship, together with his exceptional athletic prowess and strength of character, has made "Sir Donald Bradman" one of the most admired figures in the history of sports and someone worth talking about.

Instead of announcing their intended impact, your ExCo members should create impact that others feel. This is an important key in selecting your ExCo. Do you and others feel that these people consistently create the right impact with their results, regardless of what they say in their own press releases?

Results are carefully guarded through personal ownership and individual delivery. Once someone owns the actual delivery of the agreed-upon outcomes, the results speak for themselves and the fingerprints of accountability are undeniable. Consistent results at this level are rarely achieved by one person, but rather by a team. That is another reason that careful selection of your ExCo is critical. It is uncommon for a B player to attract or retain an A player (unless

the A player intends to displace him). If you have B players on your
ExCo, they will leak talent—perhaps causing you or other A players
to work around them to retain top people. This is a very inefficient
use of precious time, and yet another thing that can pull you into
working *in* the business, not *on* it.

A players know they must build capacity with other A players
in order to challenge themselves and get the results that fuel
their ambition. They are not afraid of working with people who
are better than they are. They intuitively know they can only be
lifted up if they have a solid team beneath them that can operate
independently from them. Just as you need an ExCo capable of
freeing you up, so must they build capacity so that they too can
look up to be lifted up.

Here's the rub: If, as CEO, you are a B player yourself, incapable
of providing the platform for your superstars to achieve the kinds of
results described above, they will choose to go somewhere else. Now
you are the talent leak. This is another "do not pass go" moment. Unless
you have an ExCo and the next layer full of aligned A players and
soon-to-be A players, you will be stuck *in* the business—continually
reaching down and doing others' jobs for them.

Results Principles

Diligence principles to consider when selecting your ExCo:

- If you are not freed from the day-to-day running of the
  business, you have the wrong team; educate or change them.
  The same is true for the next layer down.

- Results ≠ Execution. Reward those who demonstrate the difference, penalize those who don't.

- *Looking up* is a discipline that must be mastered in order to achieve desired results. Seek it and reinforce it.

- Capacity comes through bench strength. Lift those who have it and layer those who don't.

- Think about future fit. Determine the ability of each executive to focus *on* the business without compromising his team's efforts to focus *in* the business.

- Do they have the capacity to operate as enterprise contributors, not merely functional experts?

- Real results are always respected and undisputed by the next two layers down. Validate beyond your inner circle.

- A players can usually be spotted boldly executing the right results amid uncertainty. B players often experience paralysis.

Reputation

People's brands and reputations have always intrigued us, especially executives' perceptions of what they can or can't control about their own brand. Brands that arise from an individual's self-packaging and marketing (B-player behavior) emphasize their differentiation and personality as a product and are not always true to reality—and they rarely align with The Agenda.

A whole industry of personal brand management experts has come into being to serve high-profile people of all types. CEOs and executives are not immune to this trend, and while the efficacy of these efforts is not in question here, many executives we know have fallen into the practice of personal brand management, forgetting that *reputation* is what really counts—especially in ExCo selection. Reputation can be a litmus test for brands.

Reputations are *earned,* not engineered (this is the A-player approach). They are forged in the crucible of experience and judged by constituencies that know the value of results. This external judgment is difficult for an executive to control. Reputations are a direct reflection of the individual and are hard to fake. The good news is that reputations have a half-life, so figuring out what others really think about a potential ExCo member (whether an internal or an external candidate) is very doable. We have completed diligence on countless executives over the past couple of decades, and whether it is positive or negative, separating oneself from one's reputation is about as easy as giving your shadow the slip.

Brands are attempts to simplify complexity into something we can wrap our minds around and easily internalize for decision-making purposes. For example, do we rate someone or not? Although brands are often based on legitimate origins, they get mingled with storytelling and urban legend. We have also observed that the more senior the person we talk to, the more simplified the executive's brand becomes. It goes something like this: Tell me about …? "Nice guy, doesn't deliver." Can you add a little color please?

Then comes the executive legend, in slightly less detail than we had heard it in our previous six interviews. This is not to say that senior people are uninformed; just that they are adept at creating simplicity out of complexity in all aspects of their business. Be sure to avoid succumbing to this when it comes to the most complex part of your business—solidifying your ExCo.

Get beyond the sound bites and brands, as they may highlight the rocks you want to look under but may not help you mitigate the risks of choosing the wrong executive. And that's a mistake that can lead to a very costly divorce. Seasoned CEOs base their selection on *reputation*, investing wisely up front in trusted internal and external optics—especially in matters of the heart.

A final note on reputation: As CEO, you are probably aware of the concept of *reputational capital* as it applies to your business. It is the sum of the value of your corporate intangible assets, including patents, trademarks, business processes, quality, resilience, etc. This is a corporate asset you manage, accumulate, and trade for trust and efficacy with key stakeholders. It is exactly the same when it comes to your ExCo choices. The sum of the intangibles between you and a potential ExCo member causes an attraction that makes real alignment possible. Accumulate and manage this asset well.

Reputation Principles

Diligence principles to consider when selecting your ExCo:

- Brands and reputation are very different. Select your team based upon reputation.

- Beware of self-promotion or one-hit wonders. Select those who won't need air cover.

- Reputation and culture are shaped by what is done, *not* what is said. Believe only what you can validate.

- Reputations die hard. Do extensive diligence for internal and external options.

- Balance your gut with strong validation metrics.

- Spot opportunities to build *reputational capital* with potential ExCo members.

Alignment

Early on in the life cycle you will have removed the misaligned and laid the foundations for loyalty. In so doing, you will have pulled closest those who help you make key decisions. These people can provide you with expert knowledge or opinion that you can triangulate to make your own decisions. This is now your inner circle, recognized by all who are in the know.

With less seasoned CEOs who lack capacity in their executive, it is common for inner circles to shift and change. In order to nail the latter phase of Dilemma Two, you must establish layers one and two as your stable inner circle. In effect, your ExCo becomes your inner circle.

When we discuss this with CEOs for the first time, the majority of them do not believe it is possible. They believe the 80/20 rule applies to their ExCo—that is, 80 percent of the decisions and lifting are done by 20 percent of their ExCo. (When phrased like this, it seems a pitiable ROI—and frankly, it is.) These CEOs are always surprised—and we are delighted—when the application of their own OQ brings their ExCo into their inner circle.

In our discussion of Dilemma One, we emphasized alignment, and in particular, *misalignment*. The message here builds on that principle. Once you have secured the loyal, your focus shifts to the task of pulling closer those you will be selecting for your ExCo and executive.

The key to aligning layers one and two is not theoretical but surgical, requiring tough choices. With rare exceptions, there are only two reasons an executive leaves a job: issues with his boss or genuine opportunity elsewhere. Sure, other reasons or excuses may be given, but our experience has been that key departures always come down to this important relationship.

Covert misalignment looks like this: "I am not going to tell anyone because it will be career suicide." This attitude generates internal noise, confuses resources, clouds prioritization, and frankly, takes the hard-earned energy out of all your work.

Real alignment looks like this: "I love where we're going and believe in my boss and colleagues." This attitude generates self-perpetuating energy. There is a direct correlation between connection to purpose and an individual's ability to consistently bring his best and most creative self to organizational opportunities. Loss of executive momentum comes from disconnection with The Agenda or with you, the CEO—and that translates into a lack of drive and individual purpose and a decline in results. Nowhere are the need for attraction and desire for proximity more important than in this critical phase of selection. We only pull closest those we trust (i.e., those with whom we have high relational capital) and believe are A players (i.e., those who are competent and loyal) or soon will be.

**

While many companies strive to secure and cultivate closely-knit inner circles of highly competent, loyal executives, few have ever pursued this agenda as single-mindedly as Hong Kong and Shanghai Banking Corporation—more familiarly known as HSBC.

HSBC's rise from parochial regional bank to the world's fourth-largest global financial institution baffled most onlookers, but it was no accident. Insiders knew that the glue that made the bank's success possible was an inner circle of aligned executives called International Officers, or IOs. As HSBC grew in stature, the IOs became the world's most powerful—and most idiosyncratic—network of leaders.

When HSBC was founded in 1865, it filled an important need: at that time Hong Kong was growing quickly into a major center of international trade, and there was a desperate need for local banking services. There were, of course, local branches of European banks, but communication was a time-consuming problem—a letter sent from Hong Kong might take up to two months to arrive in Britain.[2] The growing number of international business interests in Hong Kong needed a bank based there.

The success of HSBC may seem inevitable in hindsight, given the obvious local need for the services they provided. It was *not* inevitable, however, that the bank would still be around 150 years later, or that it would by then be the most profitable financial institution in the world. This level of success was made possible by a cadre of executives groomed for their competence and loyalty—the IOs.

The IOs were British males, hand-picked as mere boys from the finest schools in the UK and grown into HSBC's next generation of leaders and culture carriers. Following a military model, the bank housed them together in a "mess" environment, at a sort of banking finishing school called Cloudlands. Here they were inculcated with the company values of efficiency, brevity, and execution. Most importantly, the environment at Cloudlands fostered an *espirit de corps*. This tight-knit, loyal group could be deployed anytime and anywhere throughout their entire careers. In order to discourage fraud, they were limited to three-year rotations in any given location. IOs were given a great deal of decision-making autonomy, which made the bank's operations extremely efficient at a time in history when communication across thousands of miles could sometimes take weeks or months. At the IO program's peak, 350 of HSBC's 17,000 executives had come through the IO system and held all the top jobs, ensuring that the desired culture was reinforced and direction could be taken from the top and interpreted for local needs. Advances in technology eventually made things even more efficient—big decisions could be made with a phone call, and all loans anywhere on the planet could be approved by an IO within twenty-four hours.

At the peak, IO turnover was only 5 percent—and 2.5 percent of that was due to retirement—in an industry whose norm at the time was above 30 percent. This level of executive dedication provided HSBC with an invaluable competitive advantage.

Certainly the environment at Cloudlands (which closed during the 1980s) may have bred a somewhat cult-like atmosphere—IOs were not allowed to marry before the age of thirty without the chairman's permission, and were considered to be "on ice" until that time.[3] This injunction remained in place until 1989, as did a prohibition of female IOs. This atmosphere in turn may have contributed to a corporate culture that made possible the criminal money-laundering scandal of recent years (an elephant in the room that cannot go unmentioned in any serious discussion of the bank).[4] But these issues were over two decades later and are beside the point, which is that by taking pains to instill its values in a tightly-knit group of loyal executives, HSBC made itself one of the most successful financial institutions in modern history, if not *the* most successful.

* * *

When selecting for alignment, the following hierarchy is important: First, what does this executive bring to you? Next, what does he bring to the ExCo? And finally, what is his benefit to the organization? Less seasoned CEOs, to their eventual regret, prioritize this list in reverse order. The concept of *who* must apply here: Who is your primary team? You, the CEO, must be their primary focus. Above all other considerations, the role you invite them to accept must be the one that is best for the achievement of The Agenda, the one that will ultimately deliver the results you mandate. The implied message here is that their functional team is secondary to you and the ExCo. Their primary team is your team, and their secondary team is their functional team. This *must* form part of the non-negotiable accountabilities. Much as loyalty-before-competence provides you with the momentum you need, at this latter phase of the life cycle, ensuring that members of your ExCo are clear that their primary team is the ExCo itself will enable you to best leverage the collective to build capacity and win.

The process of alignment in ExCo and inner-circle selection involves deciding which loyal and competent A players will receive an informal invitation to move closer to you and be privy to the informal agenda—the plans you don't commit to paper. These invitations are extended only when you've verified the individual's reputation and have sufficient confidence in his ability to execute key initiatives appropriately and deliver the results your mandate requires. As CEO, you must carefully vet any talent you are considering pulling closer, as you know they will informally represent you, the culture you wish to instill, and The Agenda you intend the organization to pursue.

Informal invitations are a signal of welcome to the individual you wish to draw closer. They are proffered within a safe environment for mutual exploration; rarely in a formal setting. The need to act informally first is a reflection of the realities of the current world, where being explicit in these matters too early can raise erroneous expectations. You want to be very sure when you "pop the question" that you know what the answer is going to be.

Your overall aim is to turn any remaining question marks about your team into exclamation points. For that reason, most of the process of drawing someone closer must remain informal and implicit, involving a series of invitations and acceptances.

We all have been in a situation when an informal invitation was offered (remember the laws of attraction and proximity) and missed. For instance, let's say that after a team dinner, you offer a ride to a key executive you want to pull closer, with whom you want to share your *informal* agenda. He offers this tone-deaf response: "It's okay. I brought my own car. I don't want to inconvenience you."

When he turns down that opportunity to spend quality time with his CEO, what exactly is he *thinking*? This may be the only opportunity you'll have in the next month to align such individuals to your needs. If they are perceptive enough to understand this, they will jump at an opportunity to be close to you. If they miss out, it will probably cause you to question their seasoning—as you should. After all, if they are capable of missing this simple invitation, what will they miss when they are supposed to be acting on your behalf?

An informal message is an invitation; multiple accepted invitations lead to increasing alignment; greater alignment builds loyalty; and consistent loyalty leads to trust.

There are four additional benefits to implied messaging:

1 *Senior Seasoning?* It allows you to test the seniority and seasoning of the person you are considering drawing nearer. Implied messages are a means of communicating amid uncertainty and a safe way to verify reciprocation. Executive language is as different from "regular" English as French is. This tests the individual's ability to understand and his willingness to respond.

2 *In My Camp?* It allows you to ascertain relatively quickly an individual's loyalty to you and The Agenda without drawing him out in the open and exposing him.

3 *Capacity Overload?* When invitations are frequently missed, it may be a signal that an individual is too busy looking down and managing execution, and lacks capacity. Without capacity, he will *not* be able to function at a higher level. This is the very issue you wish to determine.

4 *Dating or Marriage?* Finally, if invitations are not accepted, it may reveal a mismatch of values. The invitee may indeed have the desired seasoning to recognize the invitation but is actively choosing not to respond. He may wish to avoid implying alignment due to potential reputational risk. When a known competent resource declines invitations to draw closer, the

attraction probably is not there. He doesn't want to work for you, even though he may still be committed to the business or loyal to his team (as opposed to *your* team). The mindset is "I don't mind dating you, but I don't want to marry you."

Power, the very top of the pyramid, is never meant to be shared equally across the enterprise; however, alignment to The Agenda *must* draw universal adherence and loyalty. Alignment is for everyone, but power is not. It is reserved for those whom you anoint and legitimize.

Alignment Principles

Diligence principles to consider when selecting your ExCo:

- Will your inner circle, your carefully established L1 and L2, trust this individual?

- Be conscious of proximity. Can you share your informal agenda with this person, and do you want him close to you?

- Pay attention to reputational risk. Would you be comfortable with this person as your emissary?

- Has this person chosen *your* ExCo above all other team loyalties, even to the one they lead?

- Has this person mastered the discipline of *looking up* for your informal invitations? Does he see, acknowledge, and prioritize them?

- Have your attempts to draw him closer been missed or rebuffed? Is this due to capacity, seasoning, or misalignment?

Power

Power comes in many forms, and much has been written about its use and abuse that we won't rehash here. Unlike alignment, power is a limited resource that you must distribute judiciously, now that you have earned the right to do so. Those who don't have power seem to need to vilify those who possess it. Negative and positive experiences we've all had when possessing power or lacking it have taught each of us to assess what power is, and to treasure its tangible value.

The kind of power we are talking about in OQ is *legitimate power*: having the right, the authority, the responsibility, and the resources needed to deliver to The Agenda. Legitimate power comes from the right blend of formal and informal power sanctioned by the center of power—you. Think of it as a pie that you must divide up among the big investments you have made: your ExCo choices.

Just as when you were a child on the playground, you are the team captain choosing who will be on your team and what they will do. Your diligence efforts (results, reputation, and alignment) will now pay dividends in the form of your own significant power and influence, which you must legitimize.

Just because someone has power does not mean he can use it. The process of legitimizing power requires you first to *anoint*—to bestow power on an individual so that he can act on your behalf in pursuit of The Agenda. Second, you must *decree* that this person can use that power, thus establishing the boundaries of his power and the role he will play in achieving The Agenda.

Within any organization, there is *formal power* and *informal power*. Formal power is based on competence; it is the stuff you learned at business school: organizational charts, titles, tenure, reporting lines, roles, deliverables, budget allocation, etc. Informal power is more subtle and harder to quantify, but is built on loyalty, trust, and performance. It is non-hierarchal, the stuff you learn though executive experience.

The granting of power is one of the most formidable tools that a CEO has at his disposal, and understanding the value of currencies is key to having an accurate view of where current power and influence lie across an organization. Your ability to read the shifting "tectonic plates" of power within your organization will help you determine how to provide members of your ExCo with what they need to build sustainable momentum. Legitimate power is manifest in direct proportion to proximity, in alignment to The Agenda.

The application of OQ is essential in driving organizational alignment, and ultimately, how you choose to allocate power. It tells you whom you should anoint to act on your behalf, speak with your voice, and pull others closer in order to accomplish The Agenda.

As soon as you pick your team and make a formal announcement to the organization, the broader management base will apply the lens of scrutiny. They will be observing and asking:

- Who is friends with whom, and why?

- Who are they linked to; where does trust exist?

- Who is consistently involved in the most pressing, high-visibility issues?

- Whose role has expanded or contracted?

- Who are the future players and what are they likely to do?

- Who was protected despite high-visibility mistakes?

- What key decisions have these people made?

What these scrutinizers are really asking is, how will these changes affect them? Working out who has the power, why they have it, and what they will do with it leads them either to align or not to align. This is the time to really shape culture—which is more directly influenced by what is done than what is said. Your new ExCo will carry a disproportionate amount of the weight in the establishment of *your* culture. That is why it is so critical that you populate L1 and L2 with loyal and competent A players, and that you make them your new inner circle. There is no quicker way to build capacity and set the culture you desire.

Timing

We often see CEOs get their timing wrong on culture-change initiatives. They embark on these initiatives too early (Dilemma One) in their tenure, as if to say, "I have arrived, and there is a new Sheriff in town, so pay attention …" The problem is the ones with the power are the most resistant to change, and these are his direct reports. So in an attempt to circumnavigate them, the CEO goes directly to the organization. What the organization sees is no change at the top; only lip service and a CEO trying to make a hard sell. These failed attempts always end up on the scrap heap, with employees asking, "what was that all about?". Unfortunately the silver bullet of change has been fired and cannot be shot again.

We suggest that you choose *your* ExCo (Dilemma Two), and together be the change you want to see in the organization. Then and only then send out the rallying cry to the broader organization on the new way we do things around here!

Mobilizing the organization

As we've said before, for those who get their executive selection right, mobilizing the organization happens easily and rapidly. Think about it. All the usual impediments to change have been neutralized. You have eliminated all competing or confusing agendas, brought the formal and informal agendas together, and aligned *your* competent and loyal ExCo. Power has been legitimized, and illegitimate power pockets dispersed. You've derived a double bottom-line benefit from the capacity increase in efforts focused on results, and you've raised the bar on competence. In short, the *what* and *who* are now clear, at least for your ExCo. Your goal now is to have your ExCo mobilize the organization so that business as usual becomes effortless and the process you have begun cascades. Ultimately, you will have competent, aligned employees everywhere. At this point, the adage "the fish rots from the head" positively applies to the ExCo as well as to you. As you mobilize the organization, you'll probably be faced with two intertwined challenges: employee engagement and incompetence.

A person's identity is shaped by the perceived value of his contribution to the organization. A sense of belonging is crucial in maintaining employee retention, loyalty, and engagement. Everyone knows that happy employees create happy customers. In the West, lack of employee engagement has reached epidemic proportions. More specifically, studies have shown that in the United States, less than a third of workers are engaged in their jobs.[5]

While this is a multifaceted problem, leadership must take the lion's share of the blame for this inexcusable failure. Do your employees feel a sense of belonging and engagement—or have they become a statistic? With all the change that has hit them as you have assembled your aligned ExCo, they are likely to be very unsettled, and now is the time to settle them.

As employees begin their own personal journeys toward aligning themselves with The Agenda, they will experience a greater and greater sense of belonging, because they are moving in tandem with the people around them. They know what team they are playing for, they know where the team is headed, and they understand their own roles in getting there. They are part of a bigger whole, and this is a powerful motivator for you and your ExCo to harness.

Once employees have a strong sense of belonging, mobilization is effortless. They feel the connection they crave in an otherwise increasingly isolated society. When you have people who love their work and perceive it as meaningful and valuable, it's not work so much as *purpose*. Their engagement level skyrockets, and you get the best from them, both intellectually and environmentally. If an employee is operating at top capacity, his ability to think creatively and innovate is significantly heightened. This allows him to experience greater self-expression and heightens his purposeful engagement.

In selecting and empowering your ExCo, you have set the competence bar very high. The cascading effect of this will be noticeable, and both your executive and your employees will understand that they must achieve aligned results and work with a shared purpose. No longer will you find yourself doing the job for the guy you pay to do the job; because if you do, he is the wrong guy. This change will happen naturally because your executive will require it. The outdated currencies of title and tenure will be replaced by engagement and competence. The culture of high performance, in all its transparency, will ensure that there is nowhere for the incompetent to hide. There will be room only for the fully engaged.

OQ in this context serves two key purposes: First, it is the answer to the highly motivated employee's question, "What must I do to rapidly navigate a highly competitive organization?" It teaches him, and everyone around, that true alignment can only occur if they are looking up. Second, it answers the CEO's and ExCo's burning question, "How do we rapidly identify key talent across the business and then align and mobilize a motivated workforce?"

Indicators that you are stuck in Dilemma Two

- The ExCo still includes both A and B players, slowing your pace to the lowest common denominator.

- There is a silo mentality—an inability to look up—which leads to turf wars.

- The CEO and ExCo are too focused *in* the business and not enough *on* it.

- You are losing key talent you wanted to keep—usually due to a lack of opportunity.

- Capacity generation can only come from increased resourcing.

- You can't delegate "on the business" activities to every member of the ExCo.

- There is an overreliance on key talent; everybody wants a piece of this scarce resource.

- Succession options are too few; you must continually go outside to fill key positions.

- Your stakeholders want you to stay as you are; current growth is acceptable.

- By focusing on *what* rather than *who*, you cannot deliver tomorrow's results.

Indicators that you have mastered Dilemma Two

- There is a balance of focus between *in* and *on* activities.

- Succession is not a business risk because you have identified multiple viable candidates.

- You have pulled in top industry talent at Levels 1 and 2.

- There is a tangible shift in momentum, as engagement and accountability have become prime currency.

- ExCo engagement is outside of functional disciplines.

- The nature of ExCo discussions changes from tedious updates to insights.

- The ExCo becomes a self-governing body safeguarding The Agenda and mandate.

- Marketplace excitement is being generated; your presence is being felt.

- With greater alignment and transparency of The Agenda, the ExCo is bolder in their collective leadership.

- Feedback is expected and used for course correction, not personal attacks.

- There is shared access to top talent, regardless of reporting lines.

- Ultimately, the inner circle is eliminated.

Is this where it ends?

Sadly, for far too many CEOs, this is where it ends. They never solve this particular dilemma and move on from it. Either they make it through the first half but are unable to secure enough A players to deliver their mandate, or they make it through the entire dilemma but their shareholders have become so comfortable with their performance that they want to leave things well enough alone.

If you've successfully navigated the first two dilemmas, you have built a business that can virtually take care of itself. Your ExCo members are self-directed and spend the majority of their time working *in* the business while aspiring to work *on* the business. What you once thought was impossible is now your reality, and you have generated vast capacity through the discipline of looking up. How will you use all this capacity?

The next chapter is for those who are willing to find out what is really possible.

4

The third dilemma

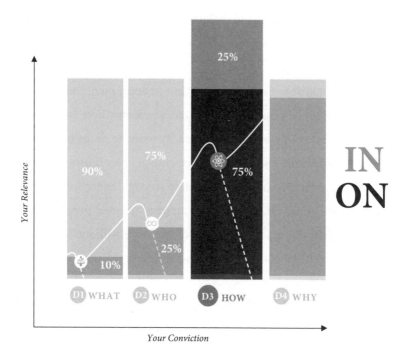

This chapter is about raising the bar of expectation and performance higher than you may currently believe possible. It is about shifting your executive from getting stuck *in* the business to working *on* the business in order to create sustainable breakthrough.

If you have mastered dilemma two, your executive will be reaching capacity for working *in* the business. You know you have the right players and there are no questions in your mind about your ExCo. These A players have mainly been focused on internal fires and fixes. They work well as a unit and have proven themselves individually and collectively. You have spent an inordinate amount of time and expended Herculean effort successfully moving through the second dilemma phase, transforming what you initially inherited into a machine that consistently delivers. The temptation is to continue to optimize efficiency gains and maintain a strong defensive team while making occasional forays into offense, quarterbacked by the MVP—you.

Things couldn't be better. You have time to think, plan, and imagine what else might be possible. Deep inside, you know there is far more to play for, but your executive is at capacity working in the business.

Do you add more horsepower by bringing in new *offensive* players? Do you use externals surgically, with deep strategic expertise? Do you create a new inner circle with more strategy-minded people? How do you satisfy the urge to push for much more without alienating the good defensive players? And most importantly, with whom do you spar?

You have arrived at Dilemma Three: **How do you engage the full capability of your executive on the business when their reputations were earned working in the business?**

Experience has taught you that when a person begins to outgrow his role, he is at risk. This becomes your reality as soon as you have a talented ExCo in place and they, in turn, have their talented reports. The real insight into this dilemma can be found in the word capability. Though your ExCo is at maximum capacity for working in the business, it is not at maximum *capability*. There exists a deep well of opportunity and growth when you switch your ExCo from defense to offense, from working at capacity *in* the business to working at capability *on* the business.

Now is the time to shift your ExCo's efforts from primarily working *in* the business to predominantly working *on* the business. This is no simple feat, as your ExCo have built their reputations by working mostly *in* the business, but it is absolutely necessary at this point in your life cycle—and it can be hugely rewarding for you and them.

The irony here is that you have little choice without churn. If the members of your ExCo are the A players we have described and you don't create a hothouse within which they can flourish, you will lose them—probably to the competition. You can be sure they will push for more: more opportunity, more responsibility, and more reward. If you simply carry on with business as usual, wringing out every last drop of incrementalism, you will create a big problem for yourself and the organization. What a great challenge to face—keeping talented, committed, and loyal players!

***

A word of caution: Market-shaping-minded CEOs may attempt to jump from Phase One (setting The Agenda) to Phase Three (sustainable breakthrough), but just because they are eager doesn't mean the organization is ready. Without the robust foundation built in Dilemma Two, you cannot lift key talent from being stuck *in* the business to get them to focus *on* the business, and break*through* becomes break*down*.

As top Finnish Formula One driver Kimi Räikkönen started the final lap of the Europe 2005 race at Nurburgring, he was roughly 1.5 seconds ahead of Fernando Alonso. While Räikkönen was braking for turn one, his vehicle's suspension collapsed under the increasing pressure, sending him spinning narrowly past Jenson Button and into the gravel trap, ending his race. Alonso was able to take the last lap easily, winning the race.

How could this have happened? Räikkönen had put a massive flat spot on his front right tire while lapping Jacques Villeneuve earlier in the race. The vibrations sustained in passing Villeneuve eventually took their toll on the suspension, causing it to fail spectacularly on the final lap. Räikkönen thus set himself up to fail at the last moment. Nevertheless, he still remained at the top of the Formula One world, which demonstrates that while not each individual risk you take works out, you remain at the top only if you do run appropriate risks.

A breakthrough isn't when your people reach an expected goal. It is when they reach a goal they never would have believed possible...thanks to your determination and their collaborative efforts. The confidence lift of an executive who delivers breakthrough results becomes infectious for the business. The appetite for sustainable breakthrough is matched only by the company's collective capability.

When faced with Dilemma Three, most CEOs do what they have always done: push the capacity button harder. This is like speaking louder and slower when a foreigner does not understand you—it doesn't get you anywhere. The secret here is in the *how*, not the *who*; it is in unlocking capability to create new capacity, and the timing couldn't be better. The momentum and drive you gained in dilemma two provide the energy you need for this next phase of the CEO's life cycle.

CEOs who know *how* to create sustainable breakthrough—and are willing to do what it takes to build a breakthrough executive and business—are outliers. They're the ones who truly shape markets. They understand that if they don't absolutely nail this dilemma, their impact will be minimized and their legacies put at risk. Unfortunately, this is also where many CEOs implode, as they confuse knowing *what* to do with *how* to do it. Not really knowing *how* to nail this dilemma can be likened to trying to guide your team to the top of Kilimanjaro. You might get there, but not without unnecessary and frankly unacceptable collateral damage.

Perhaps not really knowing *how* is also at the heart of why too many CEOs settle for marginal gains and incremental growth rather than placing the necessary focus on breakthrough. Incremental increases may serve the CEO as an individual but will rarely serve the organization over time. Timid CEOs, in their desire to protect and defend, will be out-maneuvered by the clever competition they chose to ignore. Status quo will not keep anyone in the game for long.

What type of breakthrough CEO are you?

Fortunately, a good many CEOs are up to the challenge and possess the energy required to achieve breakthrough. Unfortunately, too few can sustain that breakthrough for any meaningful length of time, as they either run out of plays or become the bottleneck.

There are many definitions for *breakthrough*. We define it as original ideas that, once executed, continue to return immense value to the organization. These ideas often redefine a marketplace and reshape current and future competition.

It is our observation that CEOs are ultimately defined by their particular strengths and ambitions; they tend to fall into three distinct camps:

1   **The Breakthrough Results CEO.** This is the most common type and potentially the most dangerous. To achieve breakthrough, this type of CEO cranks up the targets and drives the machine for results above anything else. He might be heard to say to his ExCo, "We are going for breakthrough this year, so I am going to combine your targets and multiply them by three." He is a magnet for like-minded individuals and can become an unstoppable juggernaut that no one dares to oppose. He tends to create unbalanced ExCos and cause significant business risk. When the results stop or high-profile media events occur due to cover-ups or organizational silence, high-profile resignations inevitably follow and the board is left to clean up the mess.

2   **The Breakthrough Leader CEO.** This type takes the form of the lone genius in disguise: the inventor, the engineer, the founder personality, the strategist, the dealmaker, etc. He is followed because of his absolute genius, which he can apply adeptly to create breakthrough for his organization. He often becomes a bottleneck to breakthrough as the organization has to continually take direction from him. He tends to build weak ExCos full of functional specialists or "yes men" he must

continually direct. You can easily spot this CEO, as he tends to have direct reports in the double digits. If he leaves or can no longer function, the board is forced to hire from outside the business and the new CEO will take years to rebuild.

3 **The Breakthrough Environment CEO.** This CEO is a culture carrier and protector. He is often home grown and has spent the majority of his career at the same firm, continually promoted from within. Generally, the environment and culture are stronger than he is. Usually brilliant at defense, he has a penchant for working *in* the business and a deep understanding of its people and inner workings. He typically builds collaborative and experienced ExCos with the currencies of tenure and execution. He very well may lack the skills necessary to reshape markets.

While each of these CEO types can bring about breakthrough in his own way, it is rare to find one that embodies the best qualities of all three. This significantly restricts the ability to sustain breakthrough over time. On the other hand, we have never been involved with an A player ExCo that can't be world class in all of these ways, if they know how.

Boards usually know what is needed, but the shortage of adept CEO candidates can be so frustrating that they often settle for the immediate fix when, in our opinion, a better answer is staring them in the face: what we call *sustainable breakthrough*.

As we said at the outset, it is our desire to share as much of our wisdom as possible in order to help you enhance your conviction, heighten your relevance, and actually enjoy the journey. It is therefore our intention to shine a light on what we believe is an optimal approach to creating a breakthrough ExCo—the kind that can transform your business into a market-shaping organization capable of sustaining perpetual breakthrough.

You must shift from *in* the business to *on* the business

In order to create sustainable breakthrough, you must build a breakthrough-capable ExCo. In order to have a breakthrough ExCo, you must first transition its members from working *in* the business to working *on* the business, from looking *up* to looking *out*. This requires an internal shift from your ExCo to *on* the business, an external shift to being a market-shaper, and a personal shift on your part to becoming a breakthrough-capable CEO.

As you prepare for these shifts, it goes without saying that your current modes of business—the things you do that make you money right now—must go on uninterrupted. It's not about shuttering successful businesses in the hope that something new will take their place. Instead, it's a two-track process: You keep pushing forward the things that are currently working while at the same time engaging in the discipline of creating breakthrough. Of course this is not achieved in one big jump; there must be a ratchet effect that brings you incrementally from 75 percent *in* and 25 percent *on* to exactly the reverse.

Shift 1: ExCo

In order to access the collaborative horsepower you must unleash for breakthrough results, you need to understand the transitional challenges you and your people will experience in the process so that you can create the right environment for your ExCo.

There is no shortcut. It's Napoleon to Moscow all over again. It's possible to make great time while going the wrong way. The 1929 Rose Bowl (the only bowl game there was in those days), pitted two great teams against each other: Georgia Tech and California (that's Berkeley, for those of you who aren't West Coast football fans). Roy Riegels of California recovered a fumble on Georgia Tech's 40, lost his bearings, and took off… for his own end zone. A teammate put an end to it by tackling him on the one-yard line.

The team then tried to punt but suffered a safety in the end zone (if you're not an American football fan, trust us—not good). The two points turned out to be the margin of victory in the game.

Shifting from defense to offense, as Riegels attempted to do, requires absolute clarity. Any experienced back would know instinctively that direction is more important than pace; but Riegels—a lineman attempting to step in as a running back recovering a fumble—was focused on *pace* rather than *direction*. The miscalculation was devastating.

Are you getting the point? As you transition from working *in* the business to *on* the business, it is absolutely crucial that you have invested the time and effort in mastering Dilemma Two, so the machine of capacity generation is soundly in place. The robustness of your investment in Dilemma Two allows the business to be constantly vigilant about averting potential breakdowns. As Roy Riegels painfully learned, offense may be important but it isn't in itself enough to win games. A sound defense is required as well. When Riegels seized the opportunity to perform outside his own expert function, the position was foreign to him and he failed to achieve what was possible based on the opportunity before him.

That one error earned the man a new moniker, "Wrong Way Riegels", which he bore with grace and humor for the rest of his life. You can probably think of a few CEOs who have attained their own kind of unwelcome notoriety for running in the wrong direction at pace.

It's obvious that a *breakdown* like Riegels' is quite different from a *breakthrough*. And yet, in our experience, many leaders don't fully understand what a breakthrough really is. Your real aim must be more like Nixon's when he went to China: getting people to go to a place they never in their lives imagined was possible.

The transition into breakthrough thinking is brought about by being doggedly disciplined at working *on* the business, thus challenging your executive on how they think and act. The collective expectation of breakthrough performance is that your ExCo is not tied to the day-to-day management of the business. No longer are they relentlessly working *in* the business; their time is now dedicated to determining how the enterprise will compete—which frees them up to work *on* the future of the business.

Initially unsure of how they should be contributing to working *on* the business, ExCo members may look for opportunities to get back to their comfort zone of working *in* the business. The transition to understanding the value of working *on* the business is essential, because at the initial phase, both their relevance and their conviction will fluctuate. Remember, their reputations and identities were forged while they worked *in* the business.

Here's a tip. At this point you will need to bring your executive together so you can jointly recognize—quite explicitly—what working *in* the business looked like in the past and what working *on* the business should look like now.

Even after ExCo members have accepted the need for breakthrough creation, they must still appreciate the real challenge this transition will present. As with any change, your ExCo will need to adopt a new way of thinking and behaving. In our experience, this will create tension both individually and collectively. These "transitional tensions" will challenge your ExCo to adapt to new expectations.

The following transitions are fundamental to shifting an ExCo from *in* to *on* the business:

1   From functional focus to enterprise-wide focus

2   From competitor to collaborator

3   From known to unknown

4   From expertise to contribution

5   From updates to insights

6   From results against plan to breakthrough

7   From loyalty to function to loyalty to enterprise

On the most fundamental level, there can be no difference between what you say and how you act. Your particular situation and reward structure, along with your organization's culture and currencies, will largely dictate what your ExCo will focus on. This will often require a rethinking of how best to reward them to ensure congruency.

Shift 2: Market

The external shift you need to make is from your current status to that of a market-shaper. In an effort to respond to the market and the relentless demands of intense competition, most organizations have three real options for what they will become: market protector, market driver, or market shaper. Each option is a matter of shareholder appetite, enterprise readiness, market dominance, and executive will. Each option values different organizational currencies and requires a different ExCo makeup.

A **market protector** takes a strategic approach to competition by acquiring or crushing potential threats. Its aim is to defend or buy market share. It uses its market position and size to respond to competitive challenge by acquiring new innovations and bringing the competition in house with the intent of adopting new products and services from outside in.

This is a great strategy for the acquirer, but it is generally detrimental to the acquired. The problem lies in the alignment of the acquired, which moves from a nimble, creative, and collaborative environment into an unwieldy one, where its players must fight to make even the simplest decisions. The process of acquisition and assimilation often squelches the best talent of the acquired.

This strategy works best with an ExCo that has nailed the later phase of dilemma two, adopting the mindset that "attack is the best form of defense."

In addition, the market protector must have the war chest and executive capacity to scan the market for threats and opportunities and the diligence needed to make wise acquisitions and either align them or banish them to oblivion. Breakthrough for market protectors is often defined by clever ways to preserve and extend the cash-generating potential of its portfolio of businesses and to ensure future market dominance.

A **market driver** allocates a percentage of profit into R&D, allots innovation time for employees, and attempts to target innovation surgically, through initiatives and rewards. The mindset is that if you harvest your daily yield, collective production will eventually exceed your mandate—and the off-chance strategy may even produce a golden egg.

Many CEOs tell us they are innovating because they have allocated a percentage of revenue to R&D efforts or have a dedicated function working on ideas for tomorrow. But that paradigm is the fool's gold of innovation. It allows you to keep pace with the market but rarely *shape* it. When these CEOs are asked what percentage of the ExCo's time is dedicated to innovation and working *on* the business... well, the silence can be deafening. Given the hyper-competitiveness of global markets, if an enterprise innovates only *surgically*—if it engages only in incrementalism—then it achieves only incremental gains.

Innovation in the traditional sense can only keep you in the game as it currently is. This approach produces reliable gains only until a competitor or new entrant changes the market. At that point, the enterprise is forced to go into hyper drive (demanding the ExCo's full attention) to respond and stay competitive.

This strategy is best served by a hybrid ExCo consisting of a few lone geniuses (especially the CEO) and others who play supporting roles as functional specialists. For market-driven businesses, breakthrough is often defined as finding the right "golden egg" (usually a product innovation or windfall project serving the same customer base) to promote the belief that it can bring future opportunity or returns.

A market shaper, by contrast, takes a strategic approach to building a breakthrough enterprise that *creates* the future marketplace. The CEO and his ExCo are shapers; they see themselves differently, they act and work differently, and they stay ahead of the curve by leveraging talent for breakthrough performance. They leverage the gains from dilemma two by freeing up the executive committee and CEO to work *on* the business, not *in* the business.

The future of the enterprise is not driven by the market, but rather by a deconstruction of the marketplace and a reconstruction of future competition—by envisioning what's possible. The CEO intuitively knows his organization's market-shaping potential and works to change the game and how organizations compete in it. Market shaping is the ultimate expression of *acting* rather than *being acted upon*.

This strategy is best served by a mature ExCo that is fully committed to breakthrough results and believes that its members and their colleagues can achieve such results.

It is very difficult for a market protector to alter its DNA and become a market shaper; sometimes it is easier to achieve this end via a division or sister company operating under a different brand. It is absolutely possible and highly desirable for market-driven businesses to transform into market shapers.

In addition to these traditional company approaches, Private Equity (PE) is another very important growth sector. PE often funds and ironically, mirrors the above strategies (market protectors, market drivers and in too few examples market shapers). PE funds have largely replaced the conglomerates of the 1960–1980s owning disparate businesses across sectors and continents. In our opinion, PE must learn from the mistakes of the conglomerates of the past and apply the lessons of breakthrough if they are to avoid repeating history.

Shift 3: CEO

Finally, the most important shift needs to come from you. We have never witnessed a successful transition to a market-shaping entity without the CEO's full commitment and engagement.

How would you rate your personal readiness for breakthrough? Here are some questions that will help you consider your readiness:

- Do you have enough latitude to pursue the strategy you deem most appropriate?

- If your core business ceased to provide revenue tomorrow, do you feel confident that you could respond?

- Are you confident you have Level 1 and Level 2 executives that could respond right along with you?

- Would you know *what* to do and *how* to personally lead a response to this crisis?

This situation may seem farfetched, but we all know CEOs whose businesses have disappeared seemingly overnight as a result of unforeseen circumstances. With merciless competition and markets in a state of constant turmoil, it is difficult to predict what will happen in a month, let alone three years. As one CEO recently commented, "Five years ago, I had ten competitors and I knew everything about them. Now I have fifty competitors and I know very little about them."

Here are six practical suggestions that may serve as a readiness check regarding breakthrough leadership and your role in it as CEO:

1   Own up to your responsibility to create breakthrough. Stop blaming others for your circumstances. You are free to choose; be honest with yourself.

2   Take responsibility for your own readiness. If not knowing *how* is what is stopping you, then address that problem. If you know you are not ready and can do something about that, then do it—and start now.

3   Embrace the discipline of breakthrough. Do the right things for the right reasons—not for net promoter scores or awards for being the best place in the universe to work. Sure, these have their place—but that place is back in OQ, not in breakthrough. There is a difference between exercising for the sole purpose of looking good (while still ingesting unhealthy rubbish) and exercising to stay in peak condition. You engage in breakthrough to fundamentally change the competitive landscape and to dominate. The purpose of sustainable breakthrough is to be fit for life.

4   Be very good at making—and learning from—mistakes. To
    put it bluntly, most businesses are awful at this, and ExCos
    are even worse. We preach it, but as soon as someone makes
    a mistake he is drawn and quartered. You will not create
    anything but incrementalism and fear if you cling to the
    safety of the known. Rather, you must adopt an inventor
    mindset—the belief that each failure brings you closer to a
    breakthrough. You can only break through boundaries by
    doing what no one else has ever done.

5   Accept that setbacks and surprises are part of the
    breakthrough experience. All forward motion creates
    friction; why should your situation be different? Some of
    your setbacks will result from your own poor choices and
    learning curve, others from things outside your control. A
    setback is not a sign that you are on the wrong course, but an
    opportunity to prove yourself and build your confidence. Stay
    the course.

6   Acknowledge and accept your weaknesses. No doubt they
    have been with you for a very long time and will probably
    be your companions until you die. So what? Play to your
    immense strengths and mitigate your relevant weaknesses
    through collaboration with your ExCo. The only weaknesses
    that matter are disbelief and lack of desire.

***

Even though breakthrough begins with you and readiness is a
key factor, you can engage your executive early on in this exciting
journey.

For an example of a CEO creating breakthrough, you need look no further than the world's most respected online repository of brilliant ideas, TED (Technology, Entertainment, Design).

TED began as an annual conference, but it has since expanded into a global movement with many affiliated programs. Individuals from all disciplines clamor to get their message out via the TED platform, which they know can create immediate impact.

Few know that TED has been around for over thirty years. Its real growth came only after its founder, Richard Saul Wurman, sold it to magazine publisher Chris Anderson in 2001. Anderson recognized TED's potential; the talks shared there had a potential audience far beyond the conference theater. In his words, "I've come to think that TED's mission is to address the fact that there are all these great ideas out there trapped in their silos ... Our job is to get them out of those silos and give them a chance to get to the mainstream."

Anderson and his team began posting TED Talks online for free in 2006. The move was risky—it could have alienated the conference attendees, who paid hefty fees to attend in person. But the strategy paid off, and the organization established a platform that others have since struggled to replicate.

Currently, about a three million people a day watch TED Talks online. TED's website proclaims its dedication to "ideas worth spreading." The conference is the engine, and the website is the means by which those ideas reach the world.

Some might say Anderson got lucky, but luck doesn't explain his team's sustained success. His leadership and TED's culture of innovation have enabled the organization to continually change the game. Shifting to a "not for profit" orientation allowed TED to become a "curator of ideas." Nearly half of TED's $45.1 million in revenue in 2012 came from the conferences—up from about $3 million in 2003. Attendees pay a hefty $8,500 for their tickets, but the money gets funneled into TED's other activities.

TED's speaker selection has also contributed to its success: Nowhere else will you find a former US president, a rock star, and an educator sharing the same stage. Surprisingly, however, TED's most popular speakers tend to be little known figures; for example, educator Ken Robinson's 2006 talk, "Do Schools Kill Creativity?" is viewed 500,000 times per month.

In spite of its successes, TED's rapid growth has drawn criticism. Because speakers are limited to eighteen minutes, forcing them to condense years of insight and research into a short talk, some experts say topics are being dumbed down. In response, Anderson says those critics "don't understand what we are trying to do." TED is not a university; rather, its platform is designed to connect people and start conversations.

It all began with Wurman's decision to sell to Anderson. He understood that he had grown the business to the limit of his own abilities and that it was time to turn it over to someone who could see the marketplace differently. Anderson was an inelegant novice with a clear vision of what was possible, but no idea how to get there. He was curious enough to ask questions and brave enough to push the market. Since Anderson took the helm, TED has become a talent magnet as well as a platform for shapers and thought leaders to share their ideas with a world in desperate need of them. An absolutely magnificent example of how breakthrough thinking matures to breakthrough results.

A foundation for sustainable breakthrough

Sustainable breakthrough begins with collaboration with an ExCo full of A players who are working *on* the business. If you have this, then all of you can make the journey. Your ExCo may not currently believe it is capable of breakthrough performance, but our experience suggests otherwise. It's in the *how*, not the *who*. Keep your current executives as your inner circle and use the momentum you have created to propel you on the journey together. The process may be a bit cumbersome at first, but you will be richly rewarded if you are patient.

Breakthrough works best when you share the collective goal of turning your company into a market shaper. You must be driven by a burning desire and a belief that you are capable of both imagining and creating such a reality. In short, your *New Agenda* is breakthrough, and your new prime *currency* is market-shaping value creation.

As CEO, you protect the collaborative environment and expect the ExCo to do the same. This is an element of breakthrough that requires accountability—which the executive committee generates. Creative thinking and collaboration that leads to breakthrough results must be nurtured. It is an exploratory process that involves slowing down to consider the landscape ahead and visualizing opportunities that might otherwise have gone unnoticed. If you're embracing breakthrough you're almost certainly U-turning frequently, because not all new ideas are good ideas. In a breakthrough environment, encountering dead ends on the way to innovation is expected and never penalized. Interestingly the Red Bull Rampage example we talked about earlier is grounded in a breakthrough in the bicycle industry. A group of friends began "free riding" 1940–1950s fat tired cruisers down very steep fire roads in and around Mt. Tamalpins, California. They obsessively tinkered with their bikes adding crazy things like brakes and gears, and the bikes kept evolving through continually breaking stuff. Their desire and passion for innovation eventually led them to build lighter frames with more agile geometry. Through the pioneering efforts of the innovators (Allan Bonds, Gary Fisher, Charlie Kelly, and Tom Ritchie) building better and better bikes for themselves, and other conscripts, the trend caught on and the Mountain bike was born. Though a few of these innovators profited from their efforts it was Mike Sinyard, a friend of Gary Fisher's, that took the innovators work and shaped it by building the first mass-produced mountain bike in 1981, "The Stumpjumper," for the then little known components company called "Specialized." By 1986 the mountain bike reached breakthrough proportions outselling the road bike and becoming a multibillion-dollar industry. By 1996 Mountain biking became an Olympic sport. It would be fair to say that regardless of all the innovators efforts "Specialized" would not be the market leader it is today without Mike's breakthrough leadership and vision of what was possible. Innovation on its own is rarely enough, but when combined with breakthrough leadership has the ability to shape markets and lead to massive benefits for you and your company.

You and the ExCo must create an environment in which it is understood that financial performance resulting from breakthrough ideas will occur in the future, not in the current quarter. This year's breakthrough creates next year's profit.

Breakthrough is both a process and a discipline, which means it can be learned, executed, and replicated.

Breakthrough is the process by which the enterprise embeds sustainable advantage through a systematized deconstruction of the marketplace. It accepts that the future growth of the business is not completely dependent on the resources, circumstances, or even environment of the enterprise, but rather on the collective resourcefulness of the ExCo in challenging how the business engages with the marketplace. It is a relentless quest for breakthrough creation and collaboration—things that cannot be mimicked or commoditized.

Breakthrough is a living discipline—and we use the word *discipline* because it requires discipline to transition from mastering a process to embedding a culture.

Before embarking on sustainable breakthrough, a quick sanity check should prove useful. Consider the following ExCo **Breakthrough-Readiness Indicators**:

1 Do the members of your ExCo see the need to become market shapers, and have they accepted the challenge?

2 Is your ExCo committed to moving beyond stretch targets to breakthrough targets?

3 Is your ExCo capable of operating collectively as your inner circle?

4 Have your executives removed the majority of *in*-the-business distractions?

5 Are your executives policing themselves, monitoring the transitional tensions, and actively protecting the creative environment?

6 Are your ExCo exploring breakthrough possibilities outside of their areas of functional expertise?

7 Is your ExCo becoming more flexible in its approach and more collaborative in its exploration?

8 Does your ExCo understand its creative DNA, individually and collectively?

Leveraging the full capability of your ExCo

To assist in framing the *how* of *sustainable breakthrough* and leveraging the full capability and capacity of your ExCo, the following illustration may prove useful. Tying the sustainable breakthrough outcome to the metrics of **contribution**, **performance,** and **focus** will mitigate ambiguity and facilitate a speedier, less painful transition.

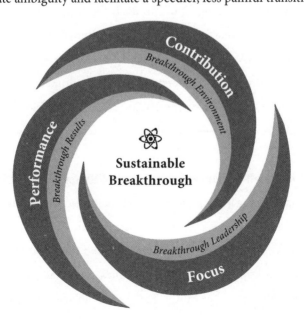

Sustainable breakthrough is the beginning of the market-shaping process; innovation focuses on the implementation of breakthrough effort. Sustainable breakthrough embraces individuals' creative traits, but unfortunately, most executives do not see or recognize their own innate creative characteristics—the very traits that will ultimately generate breakthrough results. Because creativity is rarely thought to possess hard commercial value, executives disregard their own unique creative capacity and assume their creative prowess is lacking. The truth is, conceptual skills, such as the ability to visualize patterns and synthesize abstract ideas, contribute to an atmosphere conducive to divergent thinking. Executives who understand how genuine innovation takes shape are unleashing their own creative capacity and that of the organization as a whole.

Once an executive committee has an understanding of the uniqueness of each team member's creative DNA, it can begin to leverage individual strengths within the breakthrough process. It can then establish the tone for a breakthrough culture to emerge.

Creative DNA is individual, while breakthrough DNA is a formulaic approach to understanding—and ultimately linking—the collective capability of the ExCo. This in turn will accelerate the breakthrough process, yielding the blueprint for "as needed" replication.

Breakthrough that comes as a result of collaborative effort is heavily reliant on multiple linking metrics that drive collective accountability from what *is* to what is *possible*. The first metric of breakthrough is **contribution,** the second is **performance,** and the last is **focus.** The results of breakthrough creation can be measured against the desired breakthrough targets set by the ExCo. Such metrics are individual and collective measurements, targeting both inputs and outputs of contribution, performance, and focus of the ExCo.

At the core of the illustration is the very concept of sustainable breakthrough, which can be achieved with the right inputs, outputs, and metrics.

Some believe metrics kill collaboration and creativity. Our experience with executive committees is the opposite—measurement *encourages* creativity when done properly; it directs and guides the *how* of engagement. Driving breakthrough metrics requires more than just the identification and communication of desired results. The achievement of breakthrough results requires ExCo members to have complete confidence in their collective abilities. This confidence promotes joint accountability, which eliminates distractions and drives the allocation of resources, time, and talent to the accomplishment of strategic objectives. Collective success becomes the target.

Breakthrough contribution is the metric used to represent executive contribution to breakthrough results. Capacity and capability to shape are measured by individual and collective **contribution** *on* the business. This is unfamiliar territory; historically, contribution has been based upon functional expertise and proximity to the powerbase. This is about the collective effort invested for the benefit of the enterprise.

Breakthrough contribution is inclusive of attitudes and behavior. Once individuals understand their unique creative DNA, they also understand the risks to the creative exploration process, so they bond at an attitudinal and behavioral level. In the generative process, as patterns emerge, this provides breakthrough insights.

Breakthrough contribution refutes the idea of a lone genius. You, the CEO, are not the sole proprietor of all knowledge. Your role is not to sit at an elevated vantage point from which you alone can see the next play. Breakthrough performance is about harnessing *collective* genius, beginning with the ExCo and spreading throughout the organization. The next story, about a life-saving innovation and its tortuous path to market, illustrates the point.

***

On a September morning in 1928, in the basement of St. Mary's Hospital in London, Scottish biologist Alexander Fleming noticed that one of his cultures had been contaminated by a fungus. A petri dish containing staphylococcus had been mistakenly left open beneath a window, and blue-green mold had formed a visible growth. When Fleming examined it, he noticed that a halo of inhibited bacterial growth surrounded the mold. He concluded that the mold had released a substance that repressed the growth of the staphylococci bacteria in his petri dish!

This fortuitous accident led to the development of Penicillin—used universally as an antibiotic to this day. But Fleming's astonishing discovery languished for years because his act of individual genius was not enough *in itself* to change the path of modern medicine.

Fleming was a famously poor communicator. When he presented his discovery to the Medical Research Club in London, he couldn't manage to engender much enthusiasm in his peers. Consequently, it took seventeen more years to develop a stable, mass-producible form of Penicillin. Think of the lives lost because of Fleming's shortcomings as a proponent of his own ideas, and his inability to marshal collaborators to his cause.

***

This happens every day in numerous companies around the globe, perhaps even yours. Breakthrough innovation is artificially suppressed because of inept executives and ExCos. In order to counter this tendency, we have found exponential benefit in measuring members' contributions to see, create, and deliver a creative space for exploration. A-level players who learn to collaborate bring massive value to the business. They do not lose their individuality; rather, they engage in a way that can deliver greater results than working in isolation ever could.

Informal interaction is essential for idea generation. Informal time away from day-to-day management activities is critical to breakthrough thinking and often leads to unanticipated insights. This kind of engagement requires intense interaction among ExCo members. In such a collaborative environment—outside the usual work environment—CEOs and their executives can experience the freedom to contribute as individuals, thereby consistently producing greater breakthrough results.

Contribution is ...

- The collaborative exploration of what's possible, not the defending or promoting of individual passions or pet projects.
- Collective genius, not lone genius; partnering with peers, not CEO patronage.

- Leveraging the collective creative DNA, not just mitigating individual weaknesses.

- Attitudinal and behavioral—rather than just executional—prowess; cross-disciplinary respect, not professional intolerance.

- Inquisitive novices asking tough questions, not experts feeling they need to have all the answers.

- Capability-generating, not capacity-fulfilling.

- Momentum generation and stimulating innovation, not isolated brainstorming and other momentum-destroying initiatives.

Breakthrough performance is the metric used to represent executive performance in achieving breakthrough results. It consists of a mutually agreed-upon definition of what's possible, bound by the vision of what winning looks like.

Early in the breakthrough process, the ExCo establishes targets that use prior performance as a baseline to establish agreed-upon breakthrough metrics. As one CEO put it, "In previous targeting exercises, you knew what could be comfortably done, so you built in a bit of stretch. With breakthrough, however, you commit to a goal that makes you feel nauseous when you think about it."

This is because stretch targets are based upon an instinct for where the fat is and where to tighten the belt, in order to estimate what can be delivered. The members of the ExCo each know how to achieve stretch targets—they have several "if ... then" scenarios in their back pockets, all of which would result in the achievement of "their" number.

This differs from a breakthrough approach, in which, collectively, they agree to actual breakthrough metrics without consideration of how the results are going to be achieved. The only successful path to the achievement of breakthrough results is collective commitment to the number they don't know how to deliver; anything else is not breakthrough. Simply stated, there is no banking revenue forward in the breakthrough process.

This process can be very challenging, as it introduces something most executives dread—uncertainty. Breakthrough performance requires embracing ambiguity and leaving comfort zones. Each member of the ExCo must become comfortable with ambiguity and with being an inelegant novice. As CEO, you're saying to them, "The disciplines and behaviors that have heretofore defined your careers and your remuneration—all the things that you define yourself by— aren't enough anymore."

For the process to succeed, it is important to ensure that all your ExCo members are CEO-ready. The opportunities for growth and grooming within breakthrough are a quantum of what they would receive under any other scenario. A players know this. They want a transition path that leads to commercial leadership, a path that enables them to earn the reputations they need to become successful CEOs in their own right.

Performance is also transitioning from portfolio accountability to enterprise results, thereby opening up new horizons for exploration. This is the point at which the organization fully realizes the benefit of the capacity and bench strength it has been amassing during prior CEO life cycles.

Performance is …

- Embracing uncertainty, not fearing failure; a living discipline, not a static process.

- Being an inelegant novice, not a functional expert; being CEO-ready, not a silo specialist.

- Enterprise results, not portfolio execution; doing what we say collectively, not a group of individuals saying what we've done.

- Breakthrough results, not stretch targets; committing to the near impossible, not the slightly uncomfortable.

- Repeatability and scalability, not one-off lucky breaks; collaborative capability, not professional identity.

- *How* you are creative, not *if* you are creative; organic, not linear.

- Measuring innovation against breakthrough targets, not business-as-usual metrics.

Breakthrough focus is the metric used to represent executive focus on achieving breakthrough results.

Focus is an absolute discipline; it uses one's creative DNA to see patterns and deconstruct the marketplace, exploring intuition and following instinct. Breakthrough outcomes require the executive team to look at the market in a different way and envision solutions that have not yet been designed or seen. This has never before been required of most of your ExCo members. Breakthrough performance will challenge them to become market shapers.

Most executives believe they are not naturally creative; they have defined themselves as gifted practitioners, not "creative types."

They believe creativity and intelligence are mutually exclusive—that creative types are in marketing and the softer disciplines, not central to hard data-driven business. The truth is, we are all incredibly creative and intelligent, and these qualities are not opposites but twins. It is creativity that will allow your ExCo to achieve unconventional breakthroughs.

Once an individual understands his natural creative strengths, he is able to collaborate. Cynicism and "solutioning" can kill collaborative exploration, but if these pitfalls can be avoided, there is a space for emergent thinking and exploration of what is possible. Creative collaboration promotes confidence in peer-to-peer exploration. Exploration, in turn, yields dialogue without boundaries, which presents intrigue, which invites further investigation.

Once ExCo members understand their unique individual and collective creative DNA, you can build teams that drive breakthrough time and again. This is mojo on tap. This is you, constantly living at the frontier.

Your breakthrough incubator must be protected by a disciplined focus that will not yield to any deviation that might compromise results.

Focus is …

- Transitioning to *on* the business initiatives, not retreating to *in* the business activities.

- Shaping the market, not responding to it; unique ideas that change the world, not careful refinement of what has always been done.

- Ruthless creative discipline, not brainstorming sessions; imagining possibilities, not analyzing operational viability.

- Transitioning from building capacity to leveraging capability; protecting the creative environment as the breakthrough incubator, not myopically emphasizing results.

- Transitioning from the OQ agenda to breakthrough as the *New Agenda.*

- Blowing through frequent setbacks, not laying blame for failures; shifting the collective dialogue from delivering the mandate to embedding breakthrough metrics.

Winning the war on talent using sustainable breakthrough

Consider the CEO who has just conquered Dilemma Two and is tempted to create an unofficial inner circle with a couple of fellow market shapers who can match their commercial creativity and desire for pace. *This is a tactical error we strongly caution against;* breakthrough performance MUST be engaged in by ALL of the ExCo, not a select few. When this CEO sold the vision of breakthrough to the executive in an effort to secure additional talent, these A players freed themselves up, and now they expect to shape and lead the meaningful projects. This CEO is looking for intellectual sparring partners, so he targets his creative counterparts and builds a new inner circle.

When this new inner circle is created, executives begin vying for favored status, as those who are favored lead on the most appealing and highest-impact initiatives. This leaves those who are not part of the new inner circle looking after the day-to-day management activities—running the machine—which pushes them back *in* the business, thus sacrificing the full capability of your most valued resources in favor of the few. The real issue here is one of control and confidence in the ExCo and the breakthrough process; a CEO who is unwilling to let go has now become the lone genius we referenced earlier in the chapter. It is not long before pockets of his ExCo look for opportunities elsewhere in the marketplace. Disillusioned and disenfranchised, this CEO becomes the talent leak and the bottleneck.

Once members of the ExCo have begun to model breakthrough, they must engage the rest of the talent pool. Top talent is found at all levels of the business, and talented people don't limit their collaboration and thinking to their own verticals, but are able to work across the enterprise. Breakthrough creation often comes from further down in the organization, where the talent may be less resistant to change because they are still forming their reputations and lack the attachment to incremental performance that often characterizes the old guard. In an organization in which breakthrough creation is the ultimate currency, teams will innovate so that they may rise through the ranks and challenge the old guard. These individuals tend to occupy the middle of the organization, and can model the way forward for everyone else.

Like the CEO, the executive committee cannot afford to function as a group of lone geniuses locked in their silos. They will only be able to innovate or create by maximizing the use of talent—their own and that of their teams. They must be very good at identifying, acquiring, retaining, and promoting top talent. They must also instill in their top performers the same willingness to adopt a broad range of roles.

Becoming a talent magnet

The executive world of talent acquisition, retention, and optimization has changed dramatically in the last decade. Technology has leveled much of the playing field when it comes to the expertise CEOs once relied on executives to provide: What once was specialist knowledge that executives traded off is now commoditized or can be outsourced. Organizations increasingly need CEOs and executive teams built for today's hyper-competitive world, and they are in short supply. The war for talent has really only just begun, and the next decade will see talent become the number-one competitive differentiator for organizations. Perhaps one of the greatest joys that can come from breakthrough is seeing your organization become a talent magnet, where only the best people work on the most appealing and most meaningful projects, and where there is a constant buzz and limitless opportunity. It is absolutely worth the effort, and in our opinion, the most exciting journey a market-shaping CEO can take. Market shapers never struggle with talent. Why? Because everyone wants to work for them—especially the talented!

Indicators that you are stuck in Dilemma Three

- ExCo members do not hold one another accountable for sustainable breakthrough—"That's the job of the CEO."
- Unwillingness to partner with ambiguity and move beyond established reputations.
- Retreat to the comfort of stretch targets.
- Failure to transition from *in* focus to *on* focus, from defense to offense.
- Peers are not seen as breakthrough counterparts; only as functional specialists.
- Creative talent is looking for other opportunities.
- Focus is on leveraging capacity, not releasing capability.
- A players are attracted to cash, not potential for creative expression.
- There is a constant struggle to sustain the mandate for breakthrough.
- Focus is on *who* not *how*.

Indicators that you have mastered Dilemma Three

- Focus is on collective capability, not capacity.
- The business is a talent magnet; throughout the business there is no fear of talent leak.

- ExCo engagement targets *on* the business deliverables.

- ExCo peer-to-peer engagement targets breakthrough results.

- ExCo accelerates the CEO's agenda, doesn't detract from it.

- Elimination of pre-meetings.

- ExCo success is measured by focus, contribution, and results.

- Fully engaged employee base that expects to be measured by capability.

5

The fourth dilemma

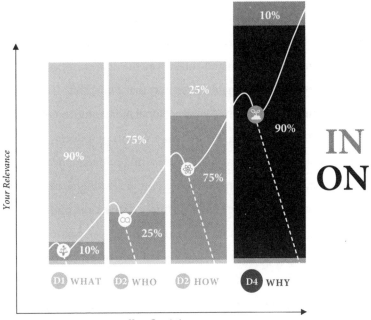

The next dilemma you face is not upwardly or outwardly focused; it is far more intimate. After focusing the enterprise on The Agenda, aligning your ExCo, and exceeding your mandate, your organization is now known for its bench strength and for achieving breakthrough results. You have an executive committee of individuals operating independently from you at peak capacity and capability, providing you both time and space for deep personal introspection—something you've not yet experienced on this journey.

Your relevance to the enterprise is no doubt very high now, and perhaps still rising. Your conviction remains high as well, but there are now many things to consider as you face the variety of opportunities that come your way. You have arrived at Dilemma Four: **At what point does the price of remaining personally relevant outweigh your other options?**

As the spotlight shines brightly—even exclusively—on you, everything becomes very real and you become almost hypersensitive. When the noise dies down and you survey the opportunities afforded you, you get a slight feeling of discomfort that something deep within you is shifting. It could be that your personal momentum has waned; it could be a niggling feeling that there is a shift in your deeply personal answer to *why* you do what you do. It is faint but uncomfortable.

Thus far, you have been too focused on generating results to look at yourself and consider your own position, desires, and options. Now is the time to reflect without the anaesthetizing perspective of *what the business needs*. Results follow the mind. You owe it to yourself not to end a vaunted career on a downhill slide. You deserve a chance to renew and rejuvenate, to accelerate your momentum and tackle this final dilemma with enthusiasm.

When your drive is aligned to your purpose and originates from your passions rather than a sense of duty, you generate momentum. You are unstoppable and bring all of your influence, contacts, experience, and skills to bear. When you're in the zone, you can change the world—and not in a small way. You are a market shaper, the mover of seemingly immovable mountains.

Until now, you have been singularly focused on getting everything and everyone to a point that few believed was possible, dismissing any distractions or dissenters along the way. Only you truly know the personal price you have paid for your success. Has it been worth it? What is next? What will it take to stay on top?

***

The question of the personal price you must pay to stay on top reminds us of a particular experience we had with a long-time client. Having worked for this chairman and his conglomerate for a number of years, we were invited to his home for a private meeting. The subject: his imminent retirement and the personal and business continuity issues this would provoke.

Over the previous two decades, he had built a conglomerate of sixteen companies, ranging from mid-cap to large-cap. He prided himself on his entrepreneurial prowess, having built each company from the ground up, from inception to execution. His style was very hands-on, with each of the portfolio companies' CEOs and CFOs reporting directly to him and his minuscule team at HQ. Everything he touched was successful, and he had earned a reputation as a leader of note in his region. Understandably, he was tired; the fire had gone, and with it his passion to carry on. This happens to many chairmen and CEOs, especially when the fun of conquering new challenges shifts to merely managing them.

As chairman and head of the family, he was conflicted. Through the years he had successfully groomed several of his siblings to run some of the portfolio companies; his exit could compromise their careers and definitely would affect their financial futures. We knew each of the family members. We had their confidence and understood the complex challenges they would face.

Our first meeting with the chairman went on into the wee hours of the morning, and mostly involved questions about his pain, motives, and plans for the future. In short, he was resolved to go for it. What followed was a series of meetings in which his siblings were encouraged to "buy in" and carve up the portfolio. It was like an intense game of monopoly being played out with real stakes, and although it was tough going, everyone aligned to the inevitable outcome.

The pivot point came one evening when we challenged the group with an alternative scenario. Now that the "sacred cow" businesses were no longer untouchable, what could be shaped from the conglomerate? Which businesses were they personally passionate about, and which less so? Which ones were the biggest drains on energy and resources and which were a pleasure to deal with? And finally, the killer (and all too often ignored) question for any conglomerate: Which businesses fit together and which ones didn't?

After several hours of robust discussion, the group began to see what we saw. The answers to those questions all centered on their health-care interests, and with some extra attention and resources, they could own the entire health-care value chain within their region. Fittingly, the chairman was passionate about his own health and that of his country. The excitement in the room was palpable as the conversation shifted from "what if" to "when" and "how"—the real Monopoly game had just begun.

Over the next few months the chairman was in fast motion. Economies of scale were identified, joint venture (JV) partners that could quickly complete the value-chain links were highlighted, boards were realigned, and non-core asset plans were put in place.

Within two years, the strategy of that pivotal night became a reality. All non-core assets had been disposed of and resources redirected toward accomplishing the new strategy. Senior mobility and brand became a strength, and synergistic savings an opportunity. The group went from being just another emerging market conglomerate to becoming one of the strongest businesses within its region. Without raising a dime of new money, the business multiplied by a factor of twenty the value of its operations. And the chairman did not retire; he recovered his energy and increased his capacity, which enabled him to spend more time with his family and pursue his other passions, including his group.

When you are feeling worn out, it is usually the noise in your life and drifting lack of passion that is at the root of the problem. Eliminate the noise; find the passion, and clarity will emerge. Your decisions determine your destiny.

***

The constant struggle of the CEO is to stay relevant, a challenge that intensifies the longer you stay in the game. In the immortal words of The Clash, the question becomes, "Should I stay or should I go now?"

The decision to stay must be an active one rather than a default, or you risk tarnishing all that you have worked to achieve. You have three real options if you feel you have run your course and are ready to pass the torch of the CEO's expansive duties to the next generation:

one option is simply to "move up," perhaps into a consulting role within the industry. Or you might take on a chairman position or fill another non-executive role on the board.

Another option is to "move out"; in other words, do the same kind of work elsewhere, taking on a new set of challenges and repeating the CEO life cycle over again. Many CEOs spend their careers doing this. Once they master the first and second phases of the CEO life cycle, they move on. They work at a succession of companies for three to five years each, turning them around and exiting with substantial remuneration. Generally, these CEOs never fully grasp the full breakthrough potential of the enterprise and never take an organization beyond the alignment and talent lift into *what's really possible.*

A third option is to "move on"—either via retirement or by making a "legacy play" in the non-profit world. CEOs who choose this option decide to use their power and influence for what they consider the greater good.

Whatever option you choose must be arrived at as a result of honest self-reflection, hyper-awareness, and the ability to look into the mirror and ask yourself some critical and probing questions about your deep and very personal *why.*

Managing your momentum

The balance of this chapter focuses on principles of personal momentum that will help you with any of the divergent roads above.

We don't mean it to be a self-help diatribe, nor a platform from which to moralize and tell you what you should do with your many talents and vast resources. We simply want to introduce the concept of "Momentum Management."

By this point, you have learned the lesson well that leadership without momentum can be a very lonely experience. There is nothing like charging ahead only to turn around and wonder why everyone else is lagging behind. The same is true with personal momentum. Obtaining, managing, and accelerating personal momentum is a critical key to leadership. With this momentum, you are unstoppable; without it, you're immobilized.

For many CEOs, the journey to the top is not unlike a trip through a hall of mirrors. Do you remember visiting this form of carnival attraction as a child? One mirror made you look short and fat, another tall and skinny, and yet another gave you the upper body of Mr. Universe. Eventually, you found the one you liked best and posed in front of it, admiring the new *you*.

CEOs are the creators and framers of their own reflections, making distortions as they see fit and the need arises. As a public figure, you contextualize and manage key messages so people see the best side. Occasionally, you must even rewrite history or listen selectively, discarding the opinions of those who are not additive or helpful. All CEOs are guilty of these things. They are far more likely to gravitate toward a pleasingly distorted mirror than to confront an accurate reflection of themselves.

When we meet with CEOs facing this final dilemma, we encourage them to ask profound and critical questions of themselves as they look directly into the undistorted mirror. How well have your thinking and habits served you over time? What are your most critical relationships and what do you do to invest in them? Do you like who you have become? What is your level of self-awareness? What do you see in your reflection? How closely aligned are your attitudes and behaviors with your internal *why*? We pose these reflective questions and others to stimulate introspection about how clearly our choices can affect the organization's momentum, and more importantly, our own.

In our experience, CEOs who have a high level of self-awareness are also those who spend time and effort recalibrating themselves, probing for any dissonance in their attitudes and behaviors under pressure. Highly self-aware CEOs *actively listen* as part of their recalibration efforts, constantly seeking additional insight that may prove a catalyst for course correction.

By contrast, CEOs possessing high levels of self-deceit often struggle to listen to others' alternative ideas of how to accomplish key aims. Even though, by virtue of their title, they have absolute accountability for the enterprise's performance, they have poor personal discipline when it comes to looking beyond their internal running narrative. They have come to believe that their perspective is superior to all others, even though it was crafted from the reflection in their own distorted mirror. This state of self-deception often goes unchecked for significant lengths of time.

How damaging is this? To use an analogy, if your plane began to fly just one degree off course when you took off from LAX, by the time you attempted to land at Charles De Gaulle in Paris you would be more than a hundred miles off course; your *Parlez-vous Français?* would become *Sprechen sie Deutsch?*

In an earlier chapter, we offered the example of an American college football player who became famous—or more accurately, infamous—for running the wrong way. What's even funnier about the story is that it is often confused with an anecdote about another fellow with a poor sense of direction—an aviator, not an athlete: Wrong Way *Corrigan*.

In 1938, Douglas Corrigan, an accomplished mechanic and pilot, flew from Long Beach, California to Floyd Bennett Field in Brooklyn, New York. He was supposed to return to Long Beach, but the inclement weather disoriented him and he ended up in Ireland.

Corrigan might have been remembered for his efforts helping to build Charles Lindbergh's Spirit of St. Louis a decade earlier. Instead, his name is synonymous with a laughable mistake (laughable only because he survived!). Even worse, thanks to a campaign manager of Richard Nixon's who got confused in his own right and told the story of "Wrong Way Riegels," he gets the blame not just for his aeronautical detour but for a disastrous run on a football field he'd never set foot on.

Unfair? Undoubtedly. But be aware that people who are remembered for errors are often blamed even for errors they did not commit. It's a slippery slope, and one best avoided.

Corrigan's was an honest mistake. He wasn't lying to himself about where he was headed; he simply had no idea he was flying east instead of west. In our experience, though, a CEO in a state of self-deception causes tremendous damage to an organization. The company's momentum can never outpace the CEO's individual momentum without becoming cannibalistic. As the ExCo begins out-pacing the CEO, the CEO may *turn on his own team*, confusing friend for foe. By the time the board comes to grips with the depth of the decay, a great deal of unnecessary damage has been done, and ultimately the board is left with no choice but to replace the CEO.

We call this form of self-deception the "King David Syndrome." Even the most moral and upright human being has flaws—chief among them the ability to lie to himself. When you tell yourself a story over and over, you start to believe it. Don't tell yourself it doesn't matter, because it does. Self-deception destroys your ability to see things clearly, and it can destroy *you* in the process. Almost every story of an industry titan's fall is the same. He starts out as an underdog, slays a few Goliaths, achieves power and prominence, believes his own spin, embraces his infallibility, stops listening to truth, and in many instances, commits an unpardonable sin. This pattern always starts with self-deception. Unfortunately, this is not Hollywood but everyday reality.

Momentum Mirror

It can be difficult to move from theoretical agreement with the concepts of momentum and truth to actually identifying and uncovering them in your life. The Momentum Mirror, if correctly applied, will generate deep insight. The wisdom gained can in turn be used as a lens to drive clarity and build and sustain momentum toward your next phase of reinvention and renewal.

Most CEOs find the Momentum Mirror incredibly helpful in assessing, measuring, and managing their personal momentum—it reflects 100 percent of themselves. The mirror illuminates the distortions that result from the stories they've told themselves over the years. Some

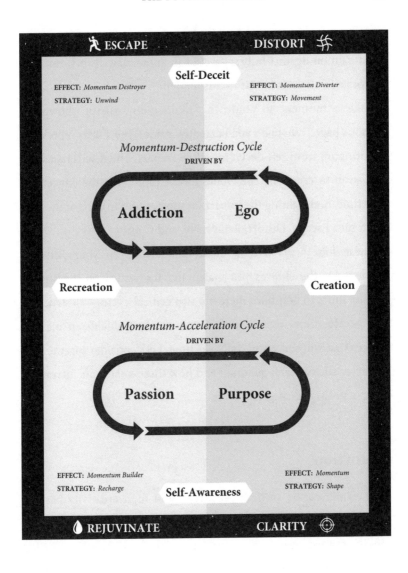

distortions are significant and others cosmetic, but they are nonetheless distortions. These well-rehearsed stories allow CEOs to bridge the gap between what they say and what they do. Unfortunately, it can become all too easy for these leaders to "believe their own press," particularly if surrounded by sycophants who sing their praises year after year.

It is important to realize that there is no moral judgment here, just a caution against hubris—we all in some way distort our own mirrors. No one is immune to this tendency.

Take a moment to study the Momentum Mirror shown on previous page. Where do you currently reside? The Y-axis represents a continuum from self-deceit to self-awareness. The X-axis measures recreation to creation. The whole model represents the entirety of your time, highlighting the impact on momentum in each of the four quadrants: Escape, Distort, Rejuvenate, and Clarity.

These four areas have a direct relationship to your personal momentum, the choices you make, and the return on investment of your time. In addition, there are two critical cycles—Destruction and Acceleration—that if understood can be valuable in making choices that will serve you well over time. Let's consider together the characteristics of each quadrant and how these quadrants interact to set up a positive or negative cycle.

Distortion

At the intersection of high self-deceit and high creativity lies the Distortion quadrant. Those who operate here are often moving rapidly toward the wrong solution and output. They are fueled primarily by personal ego, and the output of the quadrant is narcissism that diverts momentum.

When you operate out of the Distortion quadrant, you do not value others' time. You believe they are on your watch, and their time is merely an extension of your time. From this quadrant, in an effort to instill a sense of urgency, you engineer a crisis to imitate momentum. You open the door to the boardroom and throw the proverbial hand grenade on the table, spurring the ExCo into a frenzy around an engineered crisis.

Or perhaps you have witnessed Distortion's bad-boy counterfeits (swinging baseball bats in close proximity to employees; throwing reports across the room trailed by expletives, threats, and belittlement; impossible deadlines, etc.). This builds upon negative energy as you have manipulated your most valued resources for your own designs. In the Distortion quadrant, you operate from conscious deceit. You know your reflection in the mirror is distorted, but you choose to ignore the accurate image and embrace the misrepresentation. You are like Wile E. Coyote running off a cliff, comprehending the effect of gravity only as you begin to fall. Your momentum is not real; it's a desert mirage that wastes time, energy, and resources as everyone chases an illusion.

The management style associated with this quadrant is one of sheer force and determination, a proverbial grinding of the gears. You rely on relentless drive and determination; your days are typified by long working hours, and your feet are always firmly planted on the accelerator. When you operate out of this zone, you tend to burn hot and crash hard.

When functioning out of the Distortion quadrant, you frequently play roles and have a tendency to slip in and out of character depending upon the audience. Under pressure, the lines separating the real you from the actor become blurry, and your authenticity comes into question. You project inconsistency of emotional engagement and unpredictability, and these can cause your ExCo and board to distrust you.

If you cannot be yourself, you can never be your *best* self—which causes you a great deal of stress. If the problem goes unchecked, you may descend into a spiral of lost and misdirected momentum; you are measuring your progress by pace and activity rather than sustainable direction and outcomes.

To be absolutely clear on this point, it would be nearly impossible to find a CEO who does not spend vast amounts of time managing key messages to an array of stakeholders. But CEOs operating from this quadrant confuse message management with role-playing.

The questions that can help you see more clearly from this quadrant are: What churn have you experienced within your ExCo? Have you lost ExCo talent that you wanted to retain? How frequently are you given unsolicited and contrary views? When did you last embrace a direction that was not yours or one you had engineered? Do you change the energy in the room to anxious when you enter? What causes you to work from this quadrant? And what is the result for you and your stakeholders?

If you have to struggle to answer these questions, it indicates a lack of self-awareness or unconscious deceit. Take that as a warning and continue to digest this chapter in order to find your way back to self-awareness.

Escape

The Escape quadrant is driven by the habits and addictions you develop in an attempt to silence an overtaxed mind. Escape comes from a legitimate place of self-protection. We all know that if we don't turn the machine off, it will self-destruct. When you operate out of the Escape quadrant, you view time as a resource to be spent when and how you see fit. Whatever you choose to do and however you choose to spend your time blowing off steam doesn't affect anyone but you. You do not see your efforts to unwind as an investment; therefore you do not expect a return. This is often linked to the "crash hard" part of "burn hot," and destroys momentum.

Abdication is the management style associated with this quadrant. When you spend too much time in Escape, you literally become an absentee landlord, shunning your duties and responsibilities.

When you approach the need for renewal from a place of self-deceit, you may choose escapism. *After all*, you tell yourself, *I've earned it.* You seek pressure release in an effort to silence the mental chatter. Part of the challenge can be found in the descriptive word, *escape.* The feeling is, "I have to get away. I need the reprieve of mindlessness—activities that do not require me to care or think."

You engage in this quadrant with the intent to unwind, to reach a state of relaxation, but if your unwinding goes unchecked it can lead to self-harming behaviors: excessive drinking, smoking, and recreational drug use; overeating; gambling; questionable relationships, etc. These activities provide temporary reprieve and satisfy your craving for the addictive adrenaline rush.

We do not mean to make moral judgments about particular activities (although perhaps that's unavoidable for us, given the toll we've seen these behaviors take). We simply want to challenge you to avoid allowing a natural and healthy need for rejuvenation to become a habitual pressure release served by addictions that destroy personal momentum.

The pressure cooker may be too hot without your being consciously aware of it. Our experience is that the implications of residing in the Escape quadrant are farther-reaching and more limiting than CEOs initially acknowledge. Telling yourself it doesn't matter or that you will have time to make it right are symptoms of the blindness you're experiencing. Now is the time to bring this to the forefront, to examine how you unwind, and to make sure that you fully understand the implications of the habits you embrace. *Be conscious of your choices and their effect on your personal momentum.*

As with its companion, Distortion, you must ask yourself how much time you are spending operating in the Escape quadrant, and what impact that has on your personal momentum over time. Consider carefully: Do you plan how long you will spend "unwinding"? Do your favorite habits serve you well over time? What is their real impact on your self-proclaimed *why*? Are there synergies or conflicts between your purpose and how you choose to unwind?

The Momentum-Destruction Cycle

There is a self-perpetuating cycle between Escape and Distortion we call the Momentum-Destruction Cycle. Ironically, it begins early in the CEO's life cycle, with the need to establish momentum with scarce resources. What once was message management can soon become role-playing—then role adoption. With few trusted resources, you make the conscious decision to don a mask of distortion and work crazy hours, trading direction for haste in an attempt to generate momentum. You justify this by reminding yourself that it is only for a short season. While this effort may seem essential for survival and creating pace, it can take its toll on you personally, as the need for pressure-relieving escape can suck you into the vortex of "burn hot and crash hard."

A strong indicator that you are caught up in this cycle is that you are working *in* the business and never *on* the business, constantly dealing with crises and living in the weeds. Like a swimmer caught in a whirlpool, you find it very difficult to break out of this cycle without help. What was once a conscious and "temporary" choice becomes your new normal—your habitual routine. While the cycle turns, you continue to work *in* the business, never able to attract and keep the A players necessary to build sufficient capacity that you can jump off the merry-go-round.

When you are caught in the Momentum-Destruction Cycle, time is not an investment but a resource to be expended. You do not value your personal time or the time of those who support you, and this is painfully evident in your behavior and attitude. In the extreme, you completely stop listening to others, even those you know to be most important to you. You do not seek actual meaningful input, but make decisions from a position of deceit reinforced by the stories you tell yourself. The deceit inherent in this cycle of destruction is further masked by the internal conversation that tells you your chosen activities are merely a hard-earned and long overdue personal indulgence.

The Momentum-Destruction Cycle is driven by a lethal cocktail of ego and addiction, mixed with a significant deficit of self-awareness. You are almost always switched on to something, attempting to function at a minimum of 100 percent. Whether the activity is productive and helpful in generating momentum is sadly *not* the measurement for this cycle; in fact, it is actually irrelevant. The key feature of this cycle is a feeling that you must be in perpetual motion; you must feed the hungry animal. Without the diversion of perpetual motion, you will die—because quiet reflection may lead to a non-distorted view of yourself that is too painful to consider. The Momentum-Destruction Cycle perpetuates personal addiction. The narcissistic ego feeds on itself until it is totally consumed. The end result is decay.

The opportunity cost of spending too much time in this cycle is an impaired ability to discern reality in both self and others. Momentum is destroyed and the ability to sustainably create, shape, and change is nullified.

There are three ways to break this descending spiral: the CEO may be replaced, the CEO may walk out, or the CEO may recognize the peril he faces and seek outside expertise. External optics can lift his vision and address his activities, so that he can move toward the two quadrants that *produce* rather than *detract from* momentum: Rejuvenation and Clarity.

Rejuvenation

This quadrant is driven by passions that serve us well over time. When you operate out of this quadrant, your attitude toward time is one of investment. You leverage discretionary time by investing frequently in this quadrant. Purposeful rest rewards you with an increase in momentum. In this quadrant, you recharge from the pursuit of personal interests. Activities that capitalize on your down time and recreation produce purposeful rest of the mind and generate energy.

Reinvention comes from this quadrant. This is where the best breakthroughs originate. In effect, you silence your mind, temporarily suspending its normal activities, and engage the heart and body in passionate pursuits. To reward yourself for this rest, your restored mind frequently provides you with epiphanies and strokes of inspiration. Because you have built capacity, you can adopt a management style that is more reflective and packed full of insight.

The effect of investing time in this quadrant is the personal momentum that forms the foundation for reinvention through greater clarity of purpose. The strategy required here is to understand *how* to unwind. Why is one activity helpful but others harmful to momentum? When you consciously examine this quadrant, you begin to consider your objectives in Escape and match those to a point at which you have sufficiently unwound. You do not move toward checking out or indulging in potentially harmful activities.

Often we find answers in the body, by indulging in those activities we are passionate about but never have time for. What did you do before you began to climb the career ladder? Did you ski, fly planes, golf, surf, or study World War II history? Those dormant passions can be absolute momentum builders. This is not about stress management; it is about undoing years of overriding your body, of considering yourself immune to the laws of physics and living on a diet consisting solely of achievement. Your body can now lead your mind in reactivating momentum via self-awareness and exploration of the things you once cast aside.

Ask yourself these questions, and then readjust so the answers tap into the momentum you can find in this quadrant: Do I have the discipline to engage in purposeful rest of the mind? Do my passions and utilization of down time produce more energy? How much time is sufficient to consistently rejuvenate my passion and energy for the challenges ahead? Can I disassociate myself from work, in pursuit of my personal passions, long enough to recharge my batteries? Do these rejuvenating activities serve me well over time? Are there synergies between what I am becoming and where I am taking the enterprise?

Clarity

This quadrant is driven by purpose and accelerated by passions that serve you well. When you operate from this quadrant, you consider time an investment because of the consistent results it produces. This is where time invested becomes a multiplier of energy. When you are in the zone, you are at your best, shaping and enjoying the buzz that comes from creating. You are, for all intents and purposes, unstoppable.

As a CEO, you shape the world others live in, affecting everything from what they buy to how they think, even how they behave. You are not acted upon or shaped by your surroundings—you shape and act. As such, if you are not shaping, you are not fulfilled.

Ironically, in presiding over the economic growth engines that drive the free market, your responsibility to drive breakthrough results couldn't be more challenging or critical to society. As organizations and economies struggle to reinvent themselves, how can you not lead by example? Most CEOs we know possess a built-in on/off switch. You are either totally on or completely disinterested. Therefore, you need to choose wisely and from a position of self-awareness. You must be focused on things that have real meaning and purpose and remain connected to what you feel passionate about. In this quadrant, people *want* to join you on the journey. You are more positive in your interactions and relationships with others. The law of attraction comes into play: Others seek out association with you. They want to spend time with you and have positive interaction because of what they can become, not because of what you might do for them. Harnessing this attraction allows you to adopt a management style of collaboration and reap the benefits of clarity.

Consider the circumstances under which you have been the most creative. How did you get your mojo? What are the patterns you see? How can you replicate this environment? How can you tap into your creative DNA more frequently? What's possible when others want to join you on the creative journey? What else could you collectively shape and envision?

The Momentum-Acceleration Cycle

There is a self-perpetuating cycle between Rejuvenation and Clarity we call the Momentum-Acceleration Cycle. This cycle is driven by individual passion and purpose, and serves to accelerate innovative personal breakthroughs. This cycle is further underpinned by an attitude of investment, and you can expect compounding returns from time and activities within it.

To understand properly what we mean by "passion and purpose," one would do well to look to the example of Marie Curie, the early twentieth-century French physicist and chemist who was the first woman to win a Nobel Prize (and also the first person and the only woman to win a second Nobel).

Marie was born Maria Sklodowska in Warsaw, Poland, in 1867, the youngest of five children. From an early age she had a deep interest in science—perhaps an unfortunate interest, one might have thought, given a girl's prospects for a career as a scientist at the turn of the twentieth century. Higher education was unavailable to girls in Poland at that time, and her father, a physics and mathematics teacher, didn't have the financial means to pay for higher education for his daughters even if any university would have admitted them.

Maria's sister, Bronislawa, was in the same position, and the two girls resolved to support each other. Bronislawa went to Paris to study medicine while Maria worked as a tutor and nanny in order to support herself and earn extra money to send to her sister. In the evenings she studied mathematics, physics, and chemistry, and she attended lectures at Warsaw's illegal, clandestine "floating university"—the only place where a young woman could study in Poland at the time.

In 1891, the 24-year-old Maria followed her sister to Paris, where she was admitted to the prestigious Sorbonne University of Paris to study mathematics, physics, and chemistry. Because these classes were taught in French, Maria—who now called herself Marie in order to assimilate into French society—needed to learn the language quickly if she was to have any hope of keeping up with the class.

Despite her intense homesickness for her native Poland, Marie earned her master's degree in chemistry within three years, and a year later began working on her PhD in physics. It was around this time that she met and married physics professor Pierre Curie.

At this point in her education Marie Curie began to study uranium, an element whose properties were then only just beginning to be understood. Impassioned by this new field of study, Marie devoted herself to it and made numerous important discoveries about uranium and other elements that today are understood to be *radioactive*—a term Marie herself coined. During the course of her work she discovered two new elements: radium (which she found to be much more radioactive than uranium) and polonium, which she named for her native country. In 1903, at the age of thirty-four, she was awarded her PhD *and* the Nobel Prize for physics; and after her husband's death three years later, she accepted Sorbonne University's invitation to assume his position as Chair of the university's physics department. She was the first woman ever to become a professor at the University of Paris.

The odds were against Marie Curie from the beginning of her life— she was born a woman who burned from an early age with the desire to do what was then considered exclusively to be men's work. Even if she'd been a man, her father wouldn't have been able to finance the extensive education needed even to do the most ordinary, unremarkable work in her field. And Marie's work was far from ordinary.

If her gender and her economic background weren't sufficient handicaps, she faced unrelenting professional hostility from a world so steeped in sexism that there wasn't even a name for the concept at that time. When her husband was invited to give a speech about radioactivity at London's Royal Institution, Marie was not allowed to speak because she was a woman.

How did Marie surmount these barriers to her success? She was able to find the will to overcome these obstacles because science— physics, in particular—was her *passion*, and that passion gave her a deep sense of *purpose*. This depth of purpose gave her the strength she needed to put her head down and keep working. And once she was committed to her work in this way, she began to develop momentum... and that momentum ultimately made her the world's first two-time Nobel Prize winner, and one of only two scientists ever to earn Nobel Prizes in two separate disciplines.

The Momentum Acceleration Cycle relies on the capacity of the ExCo to allow time and space for the CEO to reflect and create. You are consciously working *on* the business the majority of the time. Attraction is high as direction is clear and opportunities abound, creating an environment in which A players are excelling with you.

The greatest and most successful start-ups and innovations are birthed and grown within the Momentum-Acceleration Cycle, fueled by purpose and passion. A mature CEO must learn the essential discipline of protecting rejuvenation and renewal if his goal is long-term sustainability.

We are all familiar with the power generated when we are "in the zone." This is where creation just *happens*: You don't have to think about or try to force it. You have insight and see patterns emerging without effort. Your arrival at that place doesn't have to be serendipitous; you can engineer your entrée.

When personal momentum fades, it is because we are dispassionate about the activities we are involved in or have capped our level of significance to the audience we desire to reach. As a result, personal conviction wanes. *Light on demand and heavy on supply* never ends well when viewed through the lens of commerciality. If your desire is to generate great momentum, the Momentum-Acceleration Cycle and its levers of rejuvenation and clarity are at your disposal.

Personal momentum benefits the entire enterprise. The cycle can be codified in the enterprise, resulting in significant gains in personal and collective momentum. Where creativity and innovation flow freely, CEOs can shape the future from a sustainable position of strength.

As market leaders, CEOs have an innate ability and desire to shape—but creative innovation must be the result of true personal passion. It cannot be faked. Momentum is firmly rooted in this cycle. Renewal is initiated through personal rejuvenation, and such re-creation yields innovation and creativity.

The Momentum-Acceleration Cycle allows you to exercise the option of reinvention within your current role rather than moving up into another role, moving out into a lateral role, or moving on to a non-related role. Only when you acknowledge the self-perpetuating cycle between Escape and Distortion and move into Rejuvenation and Clarity is it healthy for you to continue to lead your organization; otherwise the price you are paying for success is simply too high.

Continuous personal reinvention

CEOs who have successfully navigated Dilemmas One, Two, and Three are exceptional. The reward for recognizing and moving through each phase of the life cycle is that you are favored with the opportunity to do exactly what you want, rather than remaining stuck in the power struggles and politics that typify many organizations.

As a CEO of note, you will have many options for your future. The heart of Dilemma Four is choice. It is a simple ROI consideration, only this time it is very personal. Easy choices are easy because there is a clear winner. If the choice between moving up, moving out, moving on, or reinventing your current role is easy for you and you have a clear winner, go for it. If you are like most CEOs we encounter, however, things are not so easy. In fact, making the right choice can be downright tough.

Tough choices are tough because we have to compare multiple great options. The factors that make up tough choices are usually not equally weighted. What's more, you are not an island. The impact and/or collateral damage to those you are loyal to must be weighed and measured. As a CEO of reputation, with a significant number of great options, you know that if you get it wrong you have no one to blame but yourself. It's human nature that when we have limited options, we tend to blame others or the situation, but when we have multiple options, we blame ourselves.

In the end you have to choose the option that feels most right for you and aligns with your enduring *why*. This can be found at the intersection between what's important and what's exciting to you.

The convergence of relevance and conviction

Adhering to the principles of Renewal and Reinvention allows you to rebuild personal and collective momentum repeatedly as you advance. You thwart the Hall of Mirrors distortion by continuing to ask yourself profound and critical questions. You continually recalibrate. The ROI on this fourth dilemma is very personal, very meaningful. It's one you absolutely must get right. Reinvention and Renewal are the coordinates to the fountain of youth, and failure to locate them and move toward them can cause you to flame out in your professional and personal life.

The constant challenge of any CEO is to remain personally relevant. *Relevance is mainly driven by the ability to reinvent*: reinvent ideas, direction, and relationships—reinvent *you*. CEOs who can see change in the world and use their vantage point to both predict and shape that change can adapt continually and remain relevant.

It is only possible to operate at this level when the passion, purpose, and drive—your enduring *why*—are aligned. This is why conviction is essential to your personal momentum. *Conviction ultimately comes from the process of renewal*, as it is through renewal that we connect with our purpose and identity. Conviction becomes the fuel for the journey, and reinvention the mode of transport. Both are needed to maintain momentum as you strive to achieve your desired future.

The sacrifices you have made and the intentionality you have infused in your journey as CEO have led to the convergence of what's important (conviction) and what's exciting (relevance). This convergence gives you the power and capacity to focus where you choose. When it is led by what you find most exciting and most important, the momentum to carry it through appears.

***

Congratulations on making it this far in the book. We trust it has been an illuminating read for you, and that you have a clear sense of the Four Dilemmas and how to resolve each of them. Where do you go from here? That's the subject of our concluding chapter.

6

It's your call

In our work, we encounter CEOs as they consider their next move in light of what's really possible. We interact with those who feel deeply that there is something more to play for, something deeper to reach for, and a more perfect potential to achieve. The CEOs we serve are well paid but don't work for the money alone; to them, it is not "just a job," but a life choice. Their organizations are direct reflections of them. They feel every setback, deal with it, and overcome it. Every success is quickly celebrated so the next win can be had. It's all personal. Very personal.

These CEOs ask:

- How can I get my organization and its leaders to be more agile?

- How do I generate meaningful capacity at all levels of the organization, where capability outpaces demand?

- How do I do something that has never been done before?

- How do I leverage internal collaboration to drive external competition?

- How do I best utilize the resources at my disposal to deliver the best possible results?

- How do I leave a legacy that I am proud of and that will survive me?

- How do I meet all my commitments so I maintain integrity and credibility?

Our aim in writing this book has been to impart our wisdom to you, in the belief that it will help you enjoy the journey while ensuring that the talent and enterprise you serve are wildly successful. We hope that you've found this book an important resource, a playbook, as you consider your immediate and likely future dilemmas along with the successes you've created and will create going forward. We trust the insight you've gained will push you further into exploration and action and assist you in navigating current and future uncharted waters.

A few things we can guarantee:

- The life cycle of a CEO is real, and the dilemmas we've outlined are self-imposed ceilings.

- You have faced or will face all of these dilemmas in the course of your journey. Knowing how to accelerate through them will make the difference between being stuck *in* the business and working *on* the business.

- Misalignment is unnecessary and often fatal, while alignment is critical to your momentum and relevance.

- Momentum is your greatest ally. Every decision you make will increase or decrease its effect.

- A players have a dramatic impact on an enterprise and on the career of its CEO. Failure to engage them effectively guarantees unnecessary churn. Churn breaks momentum and compromises your journey.

- The *how* of breakthrough creation is far more important than the *who*.

- The skill set of market shaping is the best-compensated and most sought-after skill set in business.

- Alignment with your internal *why* is the root of renewal, and renewal is the enabler of conviction.

- Breakthrough is as critical to the continued success of organizations as reinvention is to you personally; reinvention is the facilitator of continued relevance.

- Creators and shapers operate best where the map ends.

Quantum shifts in the market cannot be ignored. We know that new ways of seeing your personal role and your ExCo's potential are key to negotiating these times of change and opportunity. Volatility, if seen through the appropriate lens, is a fantastic and desirable maelstrom.

We are fortunate to have had the experience that underpins this book. As you contemplate your journey and trajectory, there is an advantage in knowing definitively that there are others who have already walked this path many times.

Most of our clients run mid-cap to large-cap businesses experiencing high-growth trajectories. We aid them regardless of where they find themselves in the life cycle. We intentionally do not work with CEOs who are comfortable caretakers and prefer to maintain the status quo. We choose to take on only those whom we can help produce quanta of their current results: in other words, current and future market shapers. We specialize in massive breakthroughs and the shaping of the associated results. We are high impact and high touch, an extra pair of trusted hands to help CEOs move more smoothly through the life cycle phases they face.

As a firm of trusted advisors, we recognize that we can't possibly service such an overarching need. We have tried not to hold back, and we trust that our gift is understandable and useful in seeing both what is required and how you can advance through your particular life cycle.

What is critical now is your next move. Your next definitive step will signal what you want as a lasting legacy for yourself, your team, and your organization. Wherever you are in your life cycle, challenge yourself and your organization to get to the next level. Reach confidently for the potential that you have recognized but have not yet been able to tap into. It's your call—make it!

We wish you the best possible journey, and who knows? Perhaps one day we will meet you on the road to your continued success.

Tom, Ross, and Clifford

NOTES

An invitation

1 We use the term *CEO* to represent the most senior decision-maker in an organization and the person who bears ultimate responsibility for its people and performance.

Chapter 1

1 If at any stage you require a definition of any of the terms used in this work, please refer to the glossary at the back of the book.

2 It goes without saying that many of the CEOs we have served are women; we mean no disrespect to anyone by using the pronoun *he* throughout, strictly for consistency and ease of understanding. We look forward to a time when common usage is gender-neutral.

Chapter 3

1 Kathleen Adams et al., "Milestones," *Time*, March 4, 2001.

2 http://www.hsbc.com/about-hsbc/company-history

3 Euromoney.com, February 1997.

4 Matt Taibbi, "Outrageous HSBC Settlement ..." *Rolling Stone*, December 13, 2012.

5 http://www.gallup.com/poll/181289/majority-employees-not-engaged -despite-gains-2014.aspx

GLOSSARY OF TERMS

We know that this glossary includes many definitions and phrases that may be familiar to you. We have chosen to define both familiar and unfamiliar terms in the context of this work, and we trust this will benefit you by providing understanding and clarity.

Acceptance The act of consenting to receive an indirect request for the purpose of demonstrating alignment with or admission into a group.

Addiction A form of habitual physiological or psychological escape that negatively affects personal momentum.

Agenda The blending of the formal and the informal agendas, dictating *what* we are going to do and *how* we intend to achieve the desired results.

Alignment The discipline of looking up to understand The Agenda, what needs to be done, and how to deliver your mandate.

Ambiguity Executive uncertainty regarding role, boundaries, direction, and deliverables, usually associated with the transition from working *in* the business to working *on* the business.

Anoint To bestow legitimate power on an individual to act on behalf of the CEO in order to further The Agenda.

Belief A strongly held view or perception driven by basic human needs, manifested through day-to-day behaviors and decisions.

Belonging A basic human instinct to be a part of a collective or cause greater than oneself. Belonging is driven by internal motivators of status, contribution, and sacrifice for the benefit of self and The Agenda.

Brand To attempt to package and market one's strengths for the purpose of self and team promotion.

Breakthrough The competitive differentiator for seizing massive opportunity in order to achieve or maintain market-shaping status.

Breakthrough DNA The specific (formulaic) creative qualities of the executive team that—once recognized and unleashed—can combine to accelerate innovation and breakthrough results, yielding the blueprint for on-demand replication.

Capability The creative genius of an individual, team, or network while working *on* the business to achieve recurrent breakthrough.

Capacity The potential output of an individual, team, or network in line with delivering The Agenda. It is the precursor to being lifted up to consistently deliver the right results while working *in* the business.

CEO Life Cycle A framework and graphical representation for CEOs to understand the key dilemmas that will either prevent or accelerate his longevity and success.

Clarity A quadrant of the Momentum Mirror driven by purpose and accelerated by passions that serve us well over time.

Contribution The multiplier effect that happens to an Executive Committee when there is congruence between breakthrough thinking and synergistic behaviors.

Conviction The sum of the energy, the passion, and the purpose of a CEO as it relates to what they believe they can offer an organization.

Creative DNA The identification of the unique creative qualities of an individual that, once understood, can accelerate individual creativity and yield the blueprint for on-demand replication.

Currency Anything that is used in an organization as a medium of exchange or to increase personal power.

Decree Formal delegated authority to act on behalf of the power base.

Delivery Often confused with execution; actually the achievement of a desired result in line with The Agenda.

Discern Through the heightening of one's abilities to observe, to perceive or recognize requests or invitations and interpret unspoken messages from stakeholders. This is often linked to capacity, as time is required to look up.

Distortion A quadrant of the Momentum Mirror characterized by a tendency to see ourselves as we choose, often in conflict with reality.

Diversion The altering of the natural course of momentum caused by an inability to accurately perceive oneself as the outside world does.

Enterprise Contributor An individual who adds impact and value across the business, beyond his vertical or functional expertise.

Escape A quadrant of the Momentum Mirror driven by the habits and addictions we develop in an attempt to silence an overtaxed mind.

ExCo A commonly used acronym for the Executive Committee, comprising executive directors who are individually and collectively responsible for all aspects of the organization's strategy, operations, and decisions ensuring the organization's successful future. In the context of this work, the ExCo is also the CEO's most senior employees; a group of highly skilled, aligned, loyal, and enterprise-competent individuals who manage the pace, direction, and implementation of the CEO's mandate.

Explicit Messaging A clear statement of *what* the business intends to achieve, usually communicated formally.

Focus The multiplier effect on an Executive Committee when there is congruence between what is measured and breakthrough thinking.

Focus Metric The metric used to measure the multiplier effect present within an Executive Committee that leverages breakthrough thinking.

Formal Agenda An explicitly articulated plan of *what* results are intended, used to guide organizational activities, and hold the executive committee accountable for personal and collective success.

Functional Expert An individual who has mastered the function of his vertical responsibilities and is sought out for expert guidance and opinion.

Identity A person's positive or negative persona, as determined by his role in the workplace, which ultimately drives his behavior. Its value is driven by the external perceptions of others.

Implicit Messaging An informal method of communicating meaning used when explicit messaging would be imprudent or unwise.

Incrementalism The tendency to align thinking and actions with risk aversion. Incrementalism tends to result in steady and predictable growth, and is often adopted as a defensive mindset measured by the baseline of the market.

Influence The use of one's reputation to sway decision-making in an effort to further The Agenda.

Informal Agenda An outline, known to the inner circle, of *how* the CEO intends to organize talent and resources for the successful accomplishment of the intended results.

Invitation A formal or informal request to draw closer to the power base, often used to test an individual's seasoning or readiness to contribute to The Agenda.

Legitimate Power Having the right, the authority, the responsibility, and the resources needed to deliver to The Agenda. Legitimate power is a result of the right blend of formal and informal power sanctioned by the center of power.

Looking Down A tendency to focus *down* into the functional area and work on siloed responsibilities while remaining oblivious to the CEO's agenda.

Looking Up The ability to perceive the results the CEO is pursuing, understand why they actually matter, and see how one's own efforts can support The Agenda.

Loyalty The degree to which an individual is trusted, based on his demonstrable alignment to The Agenda. Often precursory to attraction and competence; maintained through the law of proximity.

Market-Driven A strategic approach that maintains pace with the trends and dynamics of the market through incremental innovation.

Market Protector A strategic approach to competition characterized by defending market share by acquiring or eliminating potential threats.

Market Shaper A strategic approach to building a breakthrough enterprise designed to change the nature of future competition to the organization's advantage.

Mentality The way we think individually and as an Executive Committee about breakthrough possibility.

Mid to Large Cap Sizeable businesses/entities in terms of number of of employees (typically >500) and a market capitalization typically > $2Bn.

Mobilization The deployment of loyal and talented resources engaged in interrelated and complementary efforts aligned with The Agenda.

Momentum The combined personal and collective energy creating movement toward an objective or agenda with force, speed, and accuracy.

Momentum-Acceleration Cycle A self-perpetuating cycle between Rejuvenation and Clarity that can rapidly accelerate the momentum required to deliver on the mandate.

Momentum-Destruction Cycle A self-perpetuating cycle between Escape and Distortion that can rapidly deplete the momentum required to deliver on the mandate.

Organizational Quotient (OQ) A set of formal and informal tools used by CEOs to identify alignment or misalignment in order to accelerate mobilization of the organization to The Agenda. OQ also refers to an individual's ability to discern clearly *what* needs to be done and *how* to deliver it in the right way.

Performance Metric The metric used by an Executive Committee to ensure congruence and accountability among members' behaviors and what gets measured as it relates to sustainable breakthrough.

Positive Impact The degree of influence of an individual or idea that results from a shared insight in shaping future decisions or current direction, in line with The Agenda.

Predictive Analytics Effective indicators that predict the anticipated behavior and actions of individuals, teams and organizations. The indicators are based on algorithms that identify individual and collective patterns of behavior in executive contexts. A number of variables are used and weighted in order to accurately capture the most insightful and actionable data. The analysis is displayed in a real-time dashboard to assist in assessing human capital issues (current and potential) and key areas to probe.

Recreation Activities that refresh one's mind through a conscious period of purposeful mental rest.

Reinvention Identifying core priorities and values in order to determine options (inside or outside current role) and map out personal next steps. This is best undertaken when the CEO is at or near his career peak.

Rejuvenation A quadrant of the Momentum Mirror driven by passions that serve us well over time, involving pursuits that re-energize us and renew our mental focus and strength.

Relevance The importance and value others place on an individual's contribution to achieving The Agenda. A CEO builds his relevance over the course of his tenure.

Renewal The repetitive process of restoring one's mind, body, and soul.

Reputation The judgment of various constituencies that matter regarding an individual's know-how and worthiness.

Self-Awareness The capacity for introspection, including the ability to recognize oneself as an individual, separate from the environment and others.

Self-Deceit Misperceiving oneself in a way that is personally favorable.

Signal An indication of alignment and approval/affirmation or a warning of misalignment.

Silos Vertical functions in businesses that are distinct from one another and are often operated independently, despite being conjoined within the business.

Timing A gauge of the optimal moment in which to share an insight or influence a decision that accelerates achievement of The Agenda.

Transitional Tensions In the context of breakthrough, these tensions represent the strain within the ExCo as its members transition from working *in* the business to *on* the business.

Visioning The unrestrained process of determining *what is possible*.

INDEX